The International Politics
of Marine Pollution Control

Robert A. Shinn

The Praeger Special Studies program—utilizing the most modern and efficient book production techniques and a selective worldwide distribution network—makes available to the academic, government, and business communities significant, timely research in U.S. and international economic, social, and political development.

The International Politics of Marine Pollution Control

Praeger Publishers   New York   Washington   London

PRAEGER SPECIAL STUDIES IN INTERNATIONAL POLITICS AND GOVERNMENT

Library of Congress Cataloging in Publication Data

Shinn, Robert A
    The international politics of marine pollution
control.

    (Praeger special studies in international politics
and government)
    Bibliography
    1. Marine pollution—Law and legislation.
2. Marine pollution.   3. Environmental policy.
I. Title.   [DNLM: 1. International agencies.
2. Marine biology.   3. Water pollution—Prevention
and control.   WA689 S554i 1974]
Law   341. 7'62   73-10954

PRAEGER PUBLISHERS
111 Fourth Avenue, New York, N.Y. 10003, U.S.A.
5, Cromwell Place, London SW7 2JL, England

Published in the United States of America in 1974
by Praeger Publishers, Inc.

Printed in the United States of America

This study was financed in part through a Samuel T. Arnold Fellowship from Brown University. The views and opinions expressed herein are, however, the author's own and do not reflect those of any past or present affiliation.

Most of the material was gathered from interviews, private research, and conference documentation during the period between June 1970 and May 1972. Where feasible, material has been updated through January 1973. Readers are cautioned that many excerpts and consequent analyses are based on unofficial working papers and preparatory documents, and are therefore subject to revision. The author would be grateful to receive any criticism, suggestions, and information relative to the subjects discussed.

CONTENTS

LIST OF TABLES

LIST OF FIGURES

LIST OF ABBREVIATIONS

AEC   U.S. Atomic Energy Commission

ECE   Economic Commission for Europe

EEC   European Economic Community

ENEA   European Nuclear Energy Agency

FAO   Food and Agricultural Organization

GELTSAP Group of Experts on Long-Term Scientific Policy and Planning

GESAMP Joint Group of Experts on the Scientific Aspects of Marine Pollution

GIPME Global Investigation of Pollution in the Marine Environment

IAEA   International Atomic Energy Agency

ICES   International Council for Exploration of the Sea

ICJ   International Court of Justice

ICRP   International Commission on Radiological Protection

ICSU   International Council for Scientific Unions

IGOSS Integrated Global Ocean Station System

ILC   International Law Commission

IMCO   Inter-Governmental Maritime Consultative Organization

IOC   International Oceanographic Commission

IOS   international ocean space

LEPOR Long-Term and Expanded Program of Ocean Exploration and Research

MPC   maximum permissible concentration

NATO   North Atlantic Treaty Organization

OECD   Organization for Economic Cooperation and
             Development

OCB   polychlorinated biphenyl compounds

TOVALOP Tanker Owners Voluntary Agreement Concerning
             Liability for Oil Pollution

WHO   World Health Organization

WMO   World Meteorological Organization

INTRODUCTION

Marine pollution is an international political problem of the highest magnitude but the least visibility.
It affects the health, food resources, and potential uses
of the oceans for all parts of the world. It is a global
problem interlocked with many of the great economic, political, and legal issues now before the international
community and serves as an indicator of man's ability to
adapt political institutions to technological change.

Because it has not yet received comprehensive high-
level international attention, marine pollution is one of
the most complex and least understood problems of the
twentieth century. The gaps and uncertainties of scientific knowledge in the field, the variety of chemical com-
positions and behaviors among pollutants, the numerous
pathways through which pollutants enter the marine environment, and the hard facts of economics and political interests combine to complicate and impede the growth of an
international political will to consider the question a
distinct problem of sea law. Marine pollution has, rightly or wrongly, become inexorably tied and subordinate to
other ocean issues and to the large number of proposals
for governing the sea. Obscured in debate over measures
primarily designed to regulate other activities, effective
marine pollution control may be compromised for the interests of special groups and short-term international harmony.

In this study marine pollution is isolated and identified as a distinct issue in international politics to clarify the urgency and reemphasize the desirability of its
solution. Its control is placed in perspective relative
to pollutant type and effect, to international law, and to
the various interests lobbying for change or the status
quo. This perspective provides the historical background
for analyzing organizations, forums, and proposals with
present or potential capabilities for exercising control.
The ability to regulate and reduce marine pollution is the
primary criterion for analysis; also taken into consideration are other significant factors such as apparent international acceptability, historical continuity, and practical feasibility. Final emphasis is placed on the international and domestic policy implications of the proposals

for the United States and on their effect on the future of functional internationalism.

The functions of ocean space, like the universe, are synergistic: The behavior of the whole cannot be predicted by analyzing only parts. Logically, the governance of its functions must also conform to the principles of synecology if long-term policies are to produce predicted results.*

Therefore, research designed to provide improved foundations for international public policies that influence the quality of environments must involve two broad classes of study: engineering-economic studies and institutional studies.** The first covers the development and analysis of physical, biological, and value data and is designed to provide the knowledge required to define, to the extent practicable, present conditions and future trends regarding physical environments. Institutional analysis, on the other hand, focuses on the development of laws, policies, and administrative arrangements to facilitate the realization of optimum subsystems.

Environmental policy analysts must begin to integrate the "ecological approach" to both kinds of research if they are to synthesize the likely behavior of alternative organizational patterns and to determine which overall policy frameworks merit consideration. This study takes a first step in that direction.

---

*See Harold and Margaret Sprout, An Ecological Paradigm for the Study of International Politics (Princeton, N.J.: Center of International Studies, March 1968).

**Irving K. Fox, "Research on Policy and Administration in Environmental Quality Programs," Environmental Studies, Vol. 4 (Bloomington: Indiana University Institute of Public Administration, March 30, 1967), pp. 1-14.

The International Politics
of Marine Pollution Control

1

MARINE POLLUTANTS: TYPES, SOURCES, QUANTITIES, AND EFFECTS

Proposals for the control of marine pollution are complicated by the variety of pollutants, their chemical composition and behavior, the sources and pathways by which they enter the marine environment, the nature and extent of their effects, and the degree of threat they pose over time. Some marine pollutants maintain their chemical integrity for decades and even centuries; others are degraded to harmless materials in a matter of hours or days. Certain sources of marine pollution can be pinpointed; some are subject to "probabilistic" tracing; others are, for all practical purposes, untraceable. Some pollutants present a clear and immediate threat to the marine environment and human health; others are only dangerous in long-term cumulative effects. The precise danger of many is still unknown.

This chapter summarizes the present state of general knowledge on the types, sources, quantities, and effects of the major marine pollutants. Presenting them in this fashion is arbitrary; other methods have been used with varying degrees of success.[1] No attempt has been made to discuss the scientific aspects of marine pollution in great depth; reference is made to other studies for more thorough investigation. This chapter is intended to provide the reader with a general background in order to better appreciate both the political and the scientific complexity of the problem. An understanding of the scientific aspects is a prerequisite for any useful examination of legal-political arrangements for its control.

The major categories of marine pollutants are shown in Table 1.1 and the principal sources in Table 1.2. Figure 1.1 indicates several of the more important natural factors affecting a measurement of marine pollution (dissolved oxygen concentration).

TABLE 1.1

Major Categories of Marine Pollution

Category	Harm to Living Resources	Hazards to Human Health	Hindrance to Maritime Activities	Reduction of Amenities
Domestic sewage including food-processing wastes	++	++	(+)	++
Pesticides				
Organochlorine compounds	++	(+)	--	--
Organophosphorus compounds	+	+	--	--
Carbamate compounds	+	(+)	--	--
Herbicides	+	(+)	--	--
Mercurial compounds	++	++	--	--
Miscellaneous metal-based compounds	+	+	--	--
PCBs	+	(+)	--	--
Inorganic wastes				
Acids and alkalis	(+)	--	+	--
Nutrients and ammonia	(+)	(+)	--	(+)
Cyanide	(+)	(+)	--	--
Sulfite	+	--	--	(+)
Titanium dioxide wastes	(+)	--	--	(+)
Mercury	++	++	--	--
Lead	+	+	--	--
Copper	+	?	--	--
Zinc	+	--	--	--
Chromium	+	?	--	--
Cadmium	+	?	--	--
Arsenic	+	?	--	--

Radioactive materials	--	+	--	--
Oil and oil dispersants	+	?	+	++
Petrochemicals and organic chemicals				
Aromatic solvents	+	?	--	(+)
Aliphatic solvents	+	?	--	(+)
Phenols	+	+	--	(+)
Plastic intermediates and byproducts	+	?	--	--
Plastics	(+)	--	+	+
Amines	+	?	--	--
Polycyclic aromatics	+	+	--	--
Organic wastes including pulp and paper wastes	++	?	(+)	+
Military wastes	+	?	+	?
Heat	+	--	--	--
Detergents	+	--	--	(+)
Solid objects	+	--	+	++
Dredging spoil and inert wastes	+	--	+	+

Key to symbols:
++ important
+ significant
(+) slight
? uncertain
-- negligible

3

TABLE 1.2

Principal Sources of Marine Pollution

Category of Pollutant	Manufacture and Use of Industrial Products--Disposal via Direct Outfalls and Rivers	Domestic Wastes-- Disposal via Direct Outfalls and Rivers	Agriculture, Forestry, Public Health-- Disposal via Runoff from Land
Domestic sewage including food-processing wastes	+	++	--
Pesticides			
Organochlorine compounds	+	+	++
Organophosphorus compounds	+	(+)	+
Carbamate compounds	+	--	(+)
Herbicides	+	(+)	+
Mercurial compounds	+	--	++
Miscellaneous metal-containing compounds	+	(+)	(+)
PCBs	++	(+)	--
Inorganic wastes			
Acids and alkalis	+	--	--
Sulfite	+	--	--
Titanium dioxide wastes	0	--	--
Mercury	++	+	--
Lead	+	(+)	--
Copper	++	(+)	(+)
Zinc	+	--	--
Chromium	+	--	--
Cadmium	++	--	--
Arsenic	+	--	(+)
Radioactive materials	++	--	--
Oil and oil dispersants	++	(+)	--
Petrochemicals and organic chemicals			
Aromatic solvents	++	--	--
Aliphatic solvents	+	--	--
Plastic intermediates and byproducts	++	--	--
Phenols	++	(+)	(+)
Amines	+	--	--
Polycyclic aromatics	++	--	--
Organic wastes including pulp and paper wastes	++	++	+
Military wastes	?	--	--
Heat	++	--	--
Detergents	+	++	(+)
Solid objects	+	+	--
Dredging spoil and inert wastes	+	--	--

Key to symbols:
  ++ important   -- negligible
  +   significant   0 potentially harmful
  (+) slight   * dependent on extent of weapons
  ?   uncertain   testing

Deliberate Dumping from Ships	Operational Discharge from Ships in Course of Duties	Accidental Release from Ships and Submarine Pipelines	Exploitation of Seabed Mineral Resources	Military Activities	Transfer from the Atmosphere
+	(+)	--	--	--	--
(+)	--	0	--	?	++
--	--	0	--	?	+
--	--	0	--	--	--
--	--	0	--	+	+
--	--	0	--	?	?
--	--	0	--	--	?
(+)	--	--	?	--	+
+	--	+	--	--	--
--	--	--	--	--	(+)
0	--	--	--	--	--
+	--	0	--	?	++
?	--	(+)	--	--	++
(+)	--	(+)	--	--	--
+	--	(+)	--	--	--
?	--	0	--	?	--
--	--	0	--	?	--
+	--	0	--	?	?
(+)	--	0	-	(+)	0*
+	+	++	+	+	--
(+)	--	(+)	--	?	?
(+)	--	(+)	--	?	?
+	--	(+)	--	--	?
+	--	0	--	(+)	--
(+)	--	0	--	--	--
+	--	0	?	--	--
+	--	--	--	--	--
?	?	?	--	?	--
--	--	--	--	--	--
--	--	--	--	--	--
++	++	(+)	(+)	+	--
+	--	--	++	--	--

Source: Joint Group of Experts on the Scientific Aspects of Marine Pollution, Report of the Third Session (Rome: FAO, February 1971), UN Doc GESAMP III/19, pp. 19-22.

In relation to the prevention and control of marine pollution, the symbols in Tables 1.1 and 1.2 would generally imply the following:

++ restrictive or preventive measures recommended
+ restrictive or preventive measures should be considered
0 measures to assess potential harm advisable
? further investigations required pending which caution is recommended
(+) no special action indicated
-- no special action indicated

For clarity, the "marine environment" is defined as the geographic zone seaward of the landward limit of tidal influence. This includes the seabed, the high seas, the contiguous zones, territorial waters, and estuarine zones. Although these divisions are important distinctions in economic and political discussions of the problem, they are only superficially related zones in discussions of pollutant flow and effect.

Marine pollution is defined here as the "introduction by man of substances into the marine environment resulting in such deleterious effects as harm to living resources, hazards to human health, hindrance to marine activities including fishing, impairment of quality for use of sea water and reduction of amenities."[2]

OIL AND THE HYDROCARBONS

Of all marine pollutants, oil and the hydrocarbons have received the greatest international, political, and scientific attention. As early as 1953 oil was recognized as the most destructive (gallon for gallon) of all foreign substances entering coastal water to aquatic life.[3] Of the persistent pollutants in the marine environment, oil is found in the greatest quantities.[4]

Hydrocarbons enter the marine environment from natural submarine seepage, natural decay of marine plant and animal life, shore-based industrial and transport activities (including, especially, the automobile), offshore drilling, wrecked oil tankers and other ships, and discharges from vessels that pump out cargo and ballast tanks with sea water. Submarine seeps may be controlled through "tapping" the source, but plant and marine animal decay cannot. Crude oil accounts for most of the hydrocarbons due to human activity, although fuel oils have also been spilled in great quantities. The dependence of growing

FIGURE 1.1

Factors Affecting Estuarine
Dissolved Oxygen Concentrate

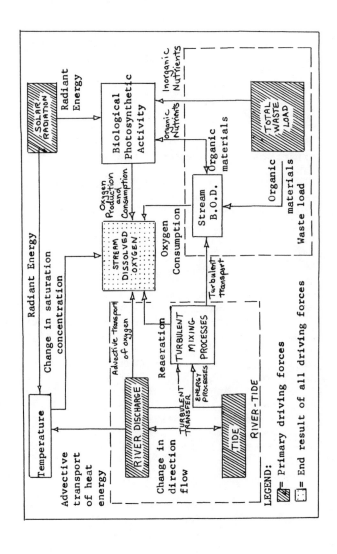

populations on a largely oil-based technology exacerbates
the growing problem since the use of oil without losses
into the environment is virtually impossible.

Recent estimates indicate that approximately 2 million
tons of oil are introduced into the oceans every year from
ocean shipping, offshore drilling, and accidents. The figures below, based on data from the federal Environmental
Protection Agency, indicate, in metric tons, the sources
and quantities of oil entering the marine environment:

Source	Tons per year	Percent of total
Used motor and industrial oil	3,300,000	67.2
Tankers (normal operations)	530,000	10.7
Other ships (bilges; oil from pleasure craft not included)	500,000	10.1
Refineries, petrochemical plants	300,000	6.0
Tanker and ship accidents	100,000	2.0
Nonship accidents	100,000	2.0
Offshore production (normal operations)	100,000	2.0
Total	4,930,000	

Shipping alone accounts for about 10^{10} grams, or about
1 million tons per year,[5] while discharges from land into
rivers account for no less than 3 million and possibly 5
million tons per annum.[6]

Although losses of oil from human activities are approximately as great as the total amount of hydrocarbons
entering the marine environment from natural plant and animal decay, they are not uniformly distributed in the world's
oceans.[7] Oil discharges in restricted shipping lanes from
standard practices, from offshore blowouts, and from massive
tanker wrecks concentrate biological effects.[8] The economics of ship routing further concentrates releases in and
around certain shipping lanes, as shown in Figure 1.2.

The ability of marine organisms to concentrate toxic
substances from a few hundred to several thousand times the
concentration in the surrounding environment compounds the
local and regional effects of oil pollution.[9]

The immediate and short-term effects of oil pollution
are obvious and well understood. Beaches used for swimming
and other recreational purposes are rendered unusable and
often subject to rapid erosion when polluted by oil. Damage to sea bird populations has been abundantly demonstrated. Of the more than 7,000 birds that were plucked
alive from the floating oil slicks caused by the notorious
Torrey Canyon disaster, it has been estimated that fewer
than 100 survived in the end.[10] Economically important
shellfish have been hurt (the oyster industry declined

FIGURE 1.2

Free World International Flow
of Petroleum, 1970

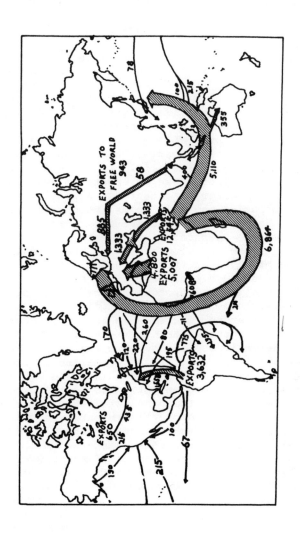

dramatically off Louisiana following the commencement of
offshore oil drilling there), and certain other sea foods
have been rendered unpalatable by oil pollution.

The biological oxygen demand (BOD) of oil is quite
high.[11] This fact indicates that waters polluted by oil
suffer decreases in dissolved oxygen vital to high-order
marine life. Most oils are broken down by microbial action, but the rate of destruction varies with the numbers
and kinds of microorganisms, with the availability of oxygen, and with temperature and form of dispersion in the
ocean. Below ten degrees centigrade, for example, bacterial oxidation is very slow; oil spilled in Arctic areas
may last as long as fifty years.[12]

While short-term toxicity for individual petroleum
fractions is available,[13] most judgments as to the long-
term effects of oil spills have been based on gross observations of acute lethalities. There is a growing amount
of evidence that these observations tell only a small fraction of the story and that the low-level effects of crude
oil pollution may well be far more serious and long-lasting
than the more obvious short-term effects. Studies by local
and federal agencies of the Santa Barbara and Gulf of Mexico offshore drilling blowouts indicated little or no evidence of any acute toxicological problems. However, they
did acknowledge the possibility of "long term ecological
effects of acute exposure to the polluting oil and the
chemical residues of the area."[14]

"The steady increase in the incidence of such patholo-
gies as cancerous lesions, leukemias, skin ulcerations,
tail deformities, and genetic changes clearly indicates
that all is not well with the marine environment."[15] Large
populations of invertebrates (such as squid) are disappear-
ing in areas where pollution is a serious problem, while in
other areas many thousands of fish display diseases that
would have been completely absent under normal circumstances. Short-term reports immediately after large oil
spills are of little consequence and misleading in their
evaluation of the real state of the environment; similarly,
spot checks do not reveal valid toxicological evaluations.

Oil pollution may have more subtle effects. Many of
the biological processes that are important for the survival of marine organisms and occupy key positions in their
life processes are mediated by extremely low concentrations
of chemical messengers in sea water. At least one study
has demonstrated that marine predators are attracted to
their prey by organic compounds at concentrations below the
part per billion level.[16] By blocking taste receptors and
mimicking natural stimuli, oil and other pollutants may

interfere with the chemical attraction and repulsion that play so important a role in finding food, in escaping from predators, in homing commercially important species, in selection of habitats, and in sex attraction.

Finally, hydrocarbons are stable, regardless of structure, once they have been incorporated into a particular marine organism. They pass through many members of the marine food chain without alteration, and in many cases they concentrate to higher levels. The stability of hydrocarbons in marine organisms is so great that hydrocarbon analysis serves as a tool for the study of marine organism food sources.[17]

In the future, larger fractions of human nutrition must be derived from the sea. At the same time, larger quantities of oil will have to be shipped by or pumped out of the sea. Tables 1.3 and 1.4 indicate the beginning of this trend as well as estimated loss directly into the world's waters in 1969.

TABLE 1.3

World Crude Oil Production and Transport by Tanker
(millions of metric tons per year)

Year	Production	Tanker Transported
1960	1,040	--
1962	1,210	--
1964	1,420	--
1965	1,500	--
1969	1,820	1,180
1975	2,700	1,820
1980	4,000	2,700

Source: Carroll L. Wilson, Man's Impact on the Global Environment (Cambridge: MIT Press, 1970), p. 266.

Marine oil transport through more hazardous waters will increase, and oil products will shift increasingly to the continental shelves and oil reserves in very deep waters.

World consumption (excluding the People's Republic of China and Warsaw Pact nations) of liquid petroleum for 1969 totaled 27,192,000 barrels per day, representing an increase in demand of 8.4 percent over 1968.[18] Growth in consumption exceeded more than 9 percent in 1970; nonsocialist countries witnessed a demand growth of almost

11

12 percent.[19] Projections for the 1980s indicate an average growth of 7 percent annually. World consumption of oil will be nearly four times that of today, use of petroleum gas five times that of today (see Table 1.5).

TABLE 1.4

Estimated Direct Oil Losses into
the World's Waters, 1969
(metric tons per year)

	Loss	Percentage of Total Loss
Tankers (normal operations)		
Controlled	30,000	1.4
Uncontrolled	500,000	24.0
Other ships (bilges, etc.)	500,000	24.0
Offshore production (normal		
operations)	100,000	4.8
Accidental spills		
Ships	100,000	4.8
Nonships	100,000	4.8
Refineries	300,000	14.4
In rivers carrying industrial		
automobile wastes	450,000	21.6
Total	2,080,000	100.0

Source: Carroll L. Wilson, Man's Impact on the Global Environment (Cambridge: MIT Press, 1970), p. 267.

World demand for petroleum (crude oil and natural gas liquids) in 1966 was 12.5 billion barrels, with approximately the following patterns of consumption:

United States	35 percent[20]
Other North America	5
Latin America	5
Europe	28
USSR	12
Africa	2
Middle East	2
Far East	11

TABLE 1.5

Forecast of Free World Energy Demand, by Component Fuels
(millions of barrels per day of oil energy
equivalent basis)

Year	Petroleum	Natural Gas	Coal	Water Power
Absolute				
1950	10.1	3.0	14.8	2.1
1965 (est.)	25.9	8.6	15.6	4.1
1975 (est.)	40.1	14.12	18.4	5.8
1985 (est.)	56.6	22.2	21.4	7.6
Percentage of demand				
1950	32.8	9.9	48.3	6.7
1965 (est.)	46.7	15.5	28.1	7.4
1975 (est.)	49.5	17.4	22.7	7.2
1985 (est.)	48.8	19.1	18.4	6.6

	Nuclear	Other	Total	
Absolute				
1950	--	0.7	30.7	
1965 (est.)	0.2	1.1	55.5	
1975 (est.)	1.8	0.8	81.0	
1985 (est.)	7.6	0.6	116.0	
Percentage of demand				
1950	--	2.3	100.0	
1965 (est.)	0.4	1.9	100.0	
1975 (est.)	2.2	1.0	100.0	
1985 (est.)	6.6	0.5	100.0	

Source: T. W. Nelson, "A Twenty Year Look at Free
World Petroleum Requirements--A 300 Billion Barrel Challenge," Journal of Petroleum Technology, 1965.

A total of 27.7 trillion cubic feet of natural gas
was marketed throughout the world in 1966 in the following pattern:

United States	62 percent[21]	
Canada	5	
Europe	9	
USSR	19	
Rest of world	5	

Total world production of oil is expected to increase
five times by 1980.[22] It has been estimated that by 1978
33 percent of the world total will come from offshore
sources; ultimate world offshore reserves are estimated to
be 1,600 billion barrels as opposed to 4,000 billion barrels from land sources.[23] By 1980 U.S. oil from foreign
sources will increase by more than 20 percent (to account
for 45 percent of the total), while offshore drilling will
produce an increase of 10 percent (30 percent of the
total).[24]

Such projections indicate the great increase of oil
flowing over and from under the sea. If care is not taken
to protect the present biological resources of the sea
from oil pollution, irreversible damages to many organisms
and to the marine food chain may occur, and the yield and
value of food from the sea may eventually be destroyed
(see Table 1.6).

TABLE 1.6

Estimated Direct Petroleum Hydrocarbon Losses
to the Marine Environment
(millions of tons)

	1969	1975 Minimum	1975 Maximum	1980 Minimum	1980 Maximum
Tankers	0.530	0.056	0.805	0.075	1.062
Other ships	0.500	0.705	0.705	0.940	0.940
Offshore production	0.100	0.160	0.320	0.230	0.460
Refinery operations	0.300	0.200	0.450	0.440	0.650
Oil wastes	0.550	0.825	0.825	1.200	1.200
Accidental spills	0.200	0.300	0.300	0.440	0.440
Total	2.180	2.246	3.405	3.325	4.752

Note: Figures do not include airborne hydrocarbons
deposited on the sea surface.

RADIOACTIVITY

Radioactivity and radioactive isotopes may enter the marine environment in the following ways: (1) from natural "background" sources; (2) from fallout of nuclear weapons testing; (3) from the operations of nuclear fission plants through intentional and unintentional direct releases; (4) from waste disposal into the sea; (5) from waste reprocessing plants; and (6) from shipborne reactors.

For the general population, the most significant amounts of radiation derive from natural background sources and medical applications. Background radiation, shown schematically in Figure 1.3, derives from cosmic rays and radioactive material naturally existing in the soil, water, and air, as well as within the human body itself. Dosage varies according to point and length of exposure. Average background levels range from 100 to 125 millirems per year.* Manmade sources of radiation include medical devices and pharmaceuticals, radiation-releasing consumer products (color television sets, luminous watches), and nuclear power facilities.

Ocean surface environmental radiation levels have declined markedly since 1963-64, due primarily to the moratorium on nuclear weapons testing in the atmosphere and underwater engendered by the acceptance of the 1963 Nuclear Test Ban Treaty (see Figure 1.4). Because of their high fission yields, long half-lives, and relative ease of determination, strontium-90 and cesium-137 are used most frequently as indicators of fallout deposition, despite the probability that more Fe-55 has been deposited on the earth's surface to date. As shown in Figure 1.5, the amount of Sr-90 on the earth's surface reached a maximum during 1966-67 and can be expected to decline exponentially with a half-life of 28 years unless atmospheric testing is resumed. The level of Cs-137 deposited is approximately 1.7 times that of Sr-90.[25]

Within the foreseeable future, however, wastes and releases from the growth of nuclear fission power plants will supersede all other sources. The production of

---

*One millirem equals 1/1,000 of a rem. Rem stands for "roentgen equivalent man" and reflects the amount of radiation absorbed in human tissues and also the quality and type of radiation.

FIGURE 1.3

Schematic Representation
of Background Radiation

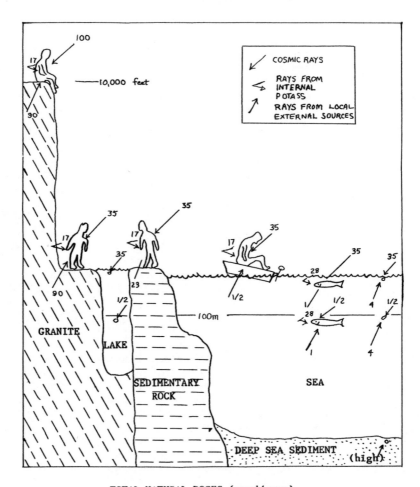

TOTAL NATURAL DOSES (mrad/year)

Man over granite		Man over sedimentary rock	Man over sea	Large fish in sea		Micro-organism in sea	
10,000 m.s.l.				at surf	100m	at surf	100m
207	142	75	52	64	30	39	5

electrical power by nuclear power plants alone is predicted to expand from about 5,000 megawatts at the end of
1968 to over 230,000 megawatts by 1980. Figure 1.6 graph-
ically depicts the various estimates of stationary nuclear
power growth to 1980. If demand for energy follows its
present pattern of doubling every thirty years, there will
be a 100 percent increase by the year 2000. Under present
technology, one megawatt-year of heat produced by a nuclear reactor results in 365 grams of fission products.
If only 10 percent of this energy demand requirement derives from fission production at 50 percent efficiency--
most experts believe nuclear power production may rise as
high as 40 percent of the total production by the year
2000--there will be a production of 1,000 to 5,000 tons
per year of waste products requiring disposal (see Tables
1.7, 1.8).[26]

FIGURE 1.4

Selected Radioactivity Trends

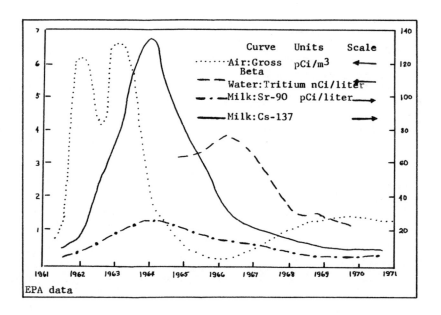

EPA data

FIGURE 1.5

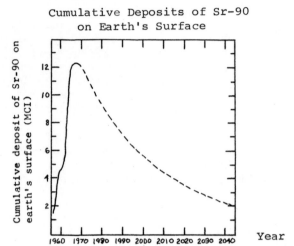

Cumulative Deposits of Sr-90
on Earth's Surface

Sr-90 reached a maximum 1967 and will decline exponentially
with a half-life of 28 years. Cs-137 is approximately 1.7
times that shown for Sr-90. The resumption of atmospheric
testing will significantly alter the projected decrease
causing upward movement to an unknown extent.

A major potential for nuclear contamination of the
environment will occur at the site of fuel-reprocessing
plants. Here, as the protective shields are removed from
containers to enable fuel recovery, fission and activated
products are exposed and the potential for escape into
the environment is increased. One estimate predicts that
99.9 percent of all radionuclides now entering the environment are released from fuel-reprocessing plants.[27]
Possible releases from this source include: I-151, Zenon-
153, Sr-90, Cs-137, H-3 (tritium), and K-85.

Although the treatment and disposal of radioactive
wastes are carefully planned at all reactor sites, the actual accepted practices vary, depending on the location
and type of reactor. Most reactors routinely release effluents containing small quantities of radioactivity into
the aquatic environment, and there have been incidents of
accidental uncontrolled releases. Nuclear reactors producing highly fissionable Pu-239 for enriched atomic fuels
and weapons have wastes similar to those produced by power
reactors; however, there are two important exceptions, the
Hanford Plant in the United States and Windscale Plant in
the United Kingdom. The first uses a single pass of Columbia River water through the reactor core for a primary
coolant, which results in an effluent containing about 60

18

FIGURE 1.6

Estimates of Stationary
Nuclear Power Growth to 1980

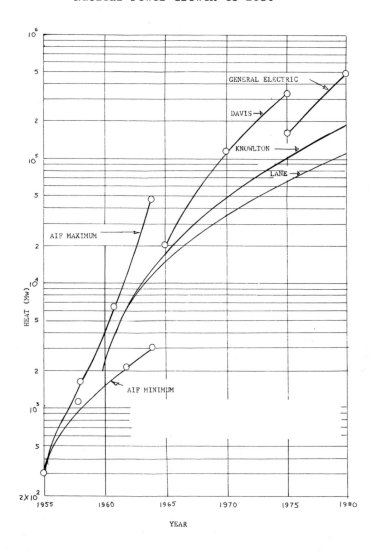

YEAR

Source: ORNL-CF-56-11-3. Basis: 25 percent efficiency in conversion of heat to electricity.

TABLE 1.7

Radioactive Wastes as a Function of Expanding U.S. Nuclear Power

	1970	1980	2000
Installed nuclear capacity, megawatts (c)	11,000	95,000	734,000
Volume high-level liquid waste[ab]			
Annual production (gallons per year)	23,000	510,000	3,400,000
Accumulated volume (gallons)[c]	45,000	2,400,000	39,000,000
Accumulated fission products, megacuries[b]			
Sr-90	15	750	10,800
Kr-25	1.2	90	1,160
H-3	0.04	3	36
Total for all fission products	1,200	44,000	860,000
Accumulated fission products (tons)	16	388	5,350

[a]Based on 100 gallons of high-level acid waste per 10,000 thermal megawatt days (MWd) irradiation.

[b]Assumes three-year lag between dates of power generation and waste production.

[c]Assumes wastes all accumulated as liquids.

Source: Snow, 1967.

TABLE 1.8

Liquid Releases from 1,000 Megawatt Nuclear Reactor

Isotope	Half-Life	Discharge Concentrations Microcuries/cc	MPC Microcuries/cc
11-3	12.3 years	3.8×10^{-6}	5×10^{-3}
Mn-54	300 days	0.8×10^{-15}	8×10^{-4}
Co-58	71 days	2.4×10^{-14}	4×10^{-4}
Co-60	5.2 years	2.9×10^{-15}	1×10^{-4}
Sr-80	50.5 days	9.8×10^{-15}	7×10^{-5}
Sr-90	27.7 years	3.0×10^{-16}	4×10^{-7}
Y-90	64.8 hours	3.4×10^{-16}	3.0
Y-91	57.5 days	1.7×10^{-14}	0.2
Mo-99	67 hours	0.7×10^{-11}	8×10^{-4}
I-151	81 days	0.6×10^{-11}	2×10^{-4}
Cs-134	2.3 years	2.1×10^{-12}	9×10^{-6}
Te-152	78 hours	0.1×10^{-12}	5×10^{-4}
I-133	20.5 hours	0.7×10^{-11}	9×10^{-4}
Cs-136	13 days	0.9×10^{-13}	9×10^{-5}
Cs-137	27 years	3.4×10^{-12}	2×10^{-5}
Ba-140	12.8 days	2.3×10^{-15}	5×10^{-4}
La-140	40.5 hours	2.1×10^{-15}	2.0
Ce-144	290 days	0.8×10^{-14}	3×10^{-2}

Source: Wright, 1970.

20

different radionuclides from leakage of fuel elements and from neutron activation within the reactor. The Windscale facility discharges about 7,500 Ci of fission products monthly about two miles offshore into the Irish Sea.[28]

The number of "contained" radioactive waste disposal operations has declined in the United States (see Table 1.9). However, there is evidence that the practice will increase from those nation-states possessing little or no land disposal sites. A number of European countries in particular have experienced difficulty in dealing with their solid radioactive wastes by burial or land storage and have engaged in "economic ocean disposal" operations.

TABLE 1.9

Radioactive Wastes Disposed at Sea:
Historical Trends, United States, 1946-70

Year	Number of Containers	Estimated Activity at Time of Disposal (in curies)
1946-60	76,201	93,600
1961	4,087	275
1962	6,120	478
1963	129	9
1964	114	20
1965	24	5
1966	43	105
1967	12	62
1968	0	0
1969	26	26
1970	2	3
Total	86,758	94,673

Sea dumping as a convenient method for disposing of radioactive wastes had its inception as far back as 1946, in infrequent garbage disposal types of operations. Drums of low-level contaminated trash were shipped out to convenient locations and put overboard.[29] Little administrative or technical control was required or exercised. The objective was to dispose of the materials as efficiently and conveniently as possible so as to eliminate the nuisance and possible hazard associated with large waste

accumulations.[30] Most of the waste during this early
period was contained in reconditioned 55-gallon drums,
many without tops, weighted with concrete or other materials to assure sinking. Figure 1.7 shows amounts disposed
and the disposal locations off the North Atlantic coast.

It has been estimated that the deposition of 1,000
tons per year of fission products (year 2000 prediction)
in the deep sea would, at secular equilibrium, almost
triple the average radiation level in deep water. Intro-
ductions of this nature could result in genetic affects
on the marine populations in these waters, which might
seriously upset the ecological system of the oceans. Contaminants could find their way back to man either directly
through accidental contact with containers washed ashore
or immersion in contaminated water above maximum permissible exposure limits, or indirectly through the consumption of living sea resources such as fish, shellfish, and
seaweed.

Tests have revealed that some sea-dwelling species
tend to concentrate a number of radioactive elements in
their bodies by factors of up to hundreds and thousands
of times the amounts of radioisotopes in the water around
them. The lowest trophic forms of sea life concentrate
certain elements by a factor of 100,000 times (see Table
1.10). Commercial fish may receive a concentrated isotope as it is passed up the food chain and provide man
with internal exposure. More physical damage results
from internal than external dosage, as certain isotopes
disfigure chemical composition patterns in the body, causing death or disease. One isotope, Sr-90, competes chemi-
cally with calcium causing bone disorders and cancer.
Iodine-131 has been connected with thyroid cancer.

The direct short-term hazards to man do not appear to
be imminent at this time from the effects of waste radioactivity in the oceans. People living and working in
coastal areas will be subject to increased radiation from
external exposure to radioactive sea water, should levels
rise, and from internal exposure from eating seafood organisms. At present levels, however, an average man would
have to eat 100 pounds of exposed fish at a sitting or as
much as ten pounds a day, day in and day out, to receive
a dose approaching danger levels.

The greatest hazards are long-term. Genetic effects
of chronic exposure to low levels of radiation are not
well understood either for marine organisms or for humans.
Unlike their terrestrial counterparts, sea organisms have

FIGURE 1.7

Past and Projected Amounts of Radioactive
Materials Disposed in Atlantic Ocean

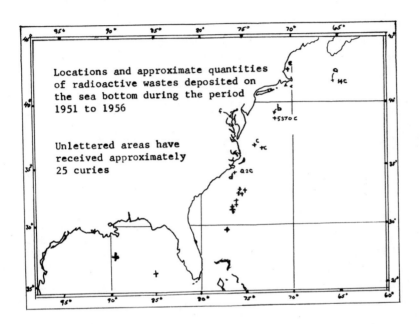

	1951–1957	Estimated 1958–63	Location (chart)
Origin			
AEC wastes (U.S. Navy Disposal)	5,370	--	a,b
Government agencies, non–AEC (U.S. Navy and Coast Guard Disposal)	4.3	531.9	b,c
University and industrial labs (Private Disposal)	10+	25+	d,e,f, and unlettered

been shielded by water from most radiation during their evolution. They are, therefore, more susceptible to radiation-induced genetic mutation. Figures 1.8 and 1.9 demonstrate the radiation sensitivities of several marine invertebrates and indicate lethal doses for different phylogenetic groups.

TABLE 1.10

Estimated Concentration Factors
in Aquatic Organisms

Radionuclide	Site	Phytoplankton	Filamentous Algae
Na-24	Columbia River	500	500
Cu-64	Columbia River	2,000	500
Rare earths	Columbia River	1,000	500
Fe-59	Columbia River	200,000	100,000
P-32	Columbia River	200,000	100,000
P-32	White Oak Lake	150,000	850,000
Sr-90/Y-90	White Oak Lake	75,000	500,000
Radionuclide	Site	Insect Larvae	Fish
Na-24	Columbia River	100	100
Cu-64	Columbia River	500	50
Rare earths	Columbia River	200	100
Fe-59	Columbia River	100,000	10,000
P-32	Columbia River	100,000	100,000
P-32	White Oak Lake	100,000	30-70,000
Sr-90/Y-90	White Oak Lake	100,000	20-30,000

Source: Eisenbud, 1963

To regulate the amount of exposure individuals should receive from radioactivity in the ocean environment, national and international authorities have established

levels of potentially harmful radioisotope dosage called
the maximum permissible concentration or MPC (see Table
1.11). Since the greatest potential hazard to man from
marine contamination is from the consumption of seafood
containing radioactivity, waste disposal into the ocean
has been regulated only to prevent the accumulation of
unsafe concentrations in edible organisms. Two divergent approaches have been developed for effecting this
control. The first establishes MPC levels according to
the critical human body organ level, that is, the safe
level to which a standard human organ that accumulates
the greatest concentration that can be accommodated of
the isotope under consideration. The body burden is the
amount of the radionuclide in the total body that produces
the maximum permissible dose to the critical organ, and
the amount allowed to be disposed (MPC) is based on the
allowable body burden. The second approach is based on
the premise that man cannot exceed his allowable body
burden of any radioisotope so long as the specific activity of that isotope in the environment is maintained
below the allowable specific activity in man.

FIGURE 1.8

Lethal Doses of Radiation
for Different Phylogenetic Groups

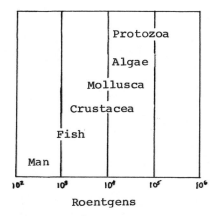

Roentgens

Lethal doses of radiation for different phylogenetic
groups. Sensitivity to radiation generally increasing
complexity of organisms. After Donaldson (1963).

25

FIGURE 1.9

Radiation Sensitivities
of Several Marine Invertebrates

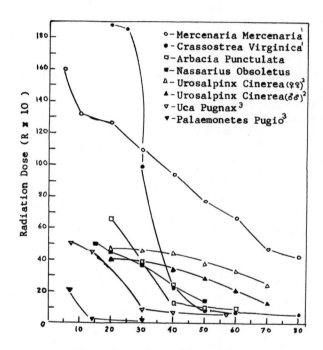

Time after irradiation (days)

Note: Shows the mean dose-time combinations at which
50 percent of the experimental animals died.
Source: White and Angelovic (1966).

TABLE 1.11

Summary of Permissible Concentrations of Selected Radionuclides in Drinking Water, Edible Marine Products, and Sea Water

	(1) Maximum Possible Concentration (microcuries/cc)	(2) Maximum Weekly Dose (microcuries)	(3) Permissible Fish Concentration (microcuries/gm)	(4) Concentration Factor	(5) Permissible Sea Concentration (microcuries/milliliter)
H-3	0.2	3,000	2	--	--
C-14	3×10^{-3}	45	3×10^{-2}	--	--
No-24	8×10^{-3}	120	8×10^{-2}	0.5	1.6×10^{-1}
P-32	2×10^{-4}	3	2×10^{-3}	4×10^4	5×10^{-8}
S-35	5×10^{-3}	75	5×10^{-2}	5	1×10^{-2}
K-42	1×10^{-2}	150	1×10^{-1}	10	1×10^{-2}
Co-45	5×10^{-4}	7.5	5×10^{-3}	10	5×10^{-4}
Cr-51	5×10^{-2}	750	5×10^{-1}	--	--
Fe-59	4×10^{-3}	60	4×10^{-2}	10^4	4×10^{-6}
Co-60	2×10^{-2}	300	2×10^{-1}	10^4*	2×10^{-5}
Cu-64	8×10^{-2}	1,200	8×10^{-1}	5×10^3	1.6×10^{-4}
Zn-65	6×10^{-2}	900	6×10^{-1}	5×10^3	1.2×10^{-4}
Sr-90	8×10^{-7}	0.012	8×10^{-6}	10	8×10^{-7}
I-131	3×10^{-5}	0.45	3×10^{-4}	100	3×10^{-6}
Cs-137	1.5×10^{-3}	22.5	1.5×10^{-2}	$50**$	3×10^{-4}
Ir-192	9×10^{-4}	13.5	9×10^{-3}	--	--

(1) Handbook 52 values (3).

(2) From MPC and weekly ingestion rate of 15 liters of water.

(3) Permissible fish concentration. From maximum weekly dose, and weekly ingestion rate of 1.5 kg of fish.

(4) The concentration factors for the soft tissues of vertebrates or invertebrates, whichever is higher, from Revelle and Schaeffer (5). In all cases, except P-32, figures are for invertebrates; vertebrates are lower by a factor of one-half to one-tenth.

*Maximum factor for plankton species. Ketchum and Bowen (in press).

**Date for soft tissues of oysters. Chipman (unpublished).

The 1959 recommendations of the International Commission on Radiological Protection (ICRP) are universally used as guides for the regulation of waste disposal (see Figure 1.10 for step by step considerations in disposal). However, each nuclear power has its own interpretations and allowable effluent levels. British policy, for example, permits greater release of radioactivity than either the United States or the USSR and requires more intensive site evaluations and environmental surveillance to ensure that the dose limitation is not exceeded. The United States allows concentrations ten times as high as those allowed by the USSR for a nuclide with a critical organ of either gonads or total body, and three times as high for other nuclides.

One well-known report indicates that if the radiation dosage "acceptable under the U.S. Atomic Energy standards were received by the total U.S. population, the results would be 32,000 extra deaths each year, from cancer and leukemia."[31] While exposure under actual operation of thermonuclear power industries is less than 1/17,000 of permitted standard, K. Z. Morgan of the Atomic Energy Commission's Oak Ridge National Laboratory has calculated that extra deaths annually due to all types of radiation-induced incidents resulting from present nuclear industry operations total about one-half of one percent of the deaths expected from exposure at the acceptable standard. This means approximately 160 people die each year due to nuclear power growth.[32] Expansion of the nuclear power industry might well take radiation exposures even beyond the present standard by the year 2000.

In October 1970 the U.S. President's Council on Environmental Quality (CEQ) recommended that:

> The current policy of prohibiting ocean dumping of high-level radioactive wastes should be continued. Low-level liquefied discharges to the ocean from vessels and land-based nuclear facilities are, and should continue to be controlled by Federal regulations and international standards. The adequacy of such standards should be continually reviewed. Ocean dumping of other radioactive wastes should be prohibited . . . ocean disposal should be allowed only when the lack of alternatives has been demonstrated. Planning of

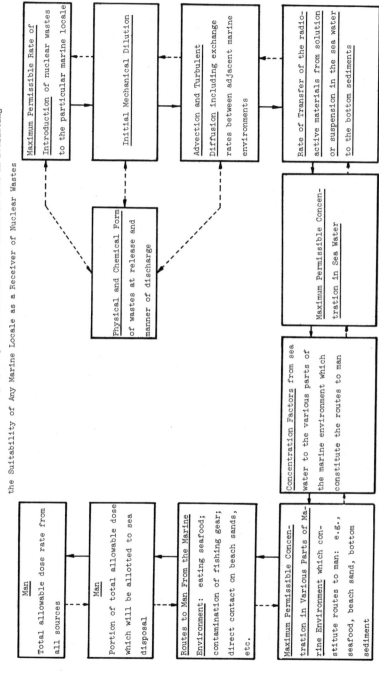

FIGURE 1.10

Schematic Presentation of the Step-by-Step Considerations that Should Be Made in Evaluating the Suitability of Any Marine Locale as a Receiver of Nuclear Wastes

activities which will involve the production of radioactive wastes should include
provisions to avoid ocean disposal.[33]

In December 1971 the United States effectively ceased to
license the sea disposal of radioactive waste, except
from the shipborne nuclear reactors of submarines. The
decision, however, was based more on the availability of
cheap land disposal sites and the passive acquiescence of
the AEC than on the CEQ recommendations.

Internationally, sea disposal has remained a live issue. The Soviet newspapers have accused the United Kingdom, France, and the United States of polluting the Atlantic. Spain and Portugal have complained that one container of a group encasing high-grade waste sunk in the
Iberian Trench 200 miles off the Portuguese coast in
waters supposed to be still was brought to the surface by
very slow upwellings and picked up by a fishing vessel
whose captain was ignorant of its contents. The United
Kingdom has continued to release liquid wastes, despite
the possible danger of accidental discharges, from its
three-mile-long pipeline at Windscale, Calder, into the
Irish Sea, basing release limits on the average consumption of Welsh laver bread made of contaminated seaweed.
In 1967-68 the European Nuclear Energy Agency (ENEA) carried out two large-scale disposal operations in the North
Atlantic totaling approximately 60,000 containers with
approximately 30,000 curies of beta/gamma activity.[34]
Japan has also carried out several rather extensive sea
disposal operations off its coast.

PESTICIDES

Pesticides represent a major category of marine pollutants, covering a wide range of substances of differing
chemical composition and classes of target organisms. Although much of the marine environmental damage caused by
organochlorine (DDT) compounds and polychlorinated byphenyl
(PCB) compounds has been widely publicized, it is often
regarded as a "land" problem, not one for the marine environment. Yet, as for most land pollutants, great quantities wash into the sea.

Much information is available on the pesticides known
as organochlorine compounds, some of which have been in
use for about thirty years.[35] DDT, BHC, Dieldren, Endrin,
Aldrin, and Endosulfan are the most commonly used as

insecticides for agricultural, military, and public health
pest control. Large-scale spraying from the air is often
the most common means of application. In some instances
less than 50 percent of the material reaches the target
area, much of it being lost to the atmosphere. Aerial
transport, in air or absorbed on airborne particulate
matter, accounts for at least 50 percent of the material
reaching the sea.[36]
    Because the organochlorine compounds are relatively
insoluble in water and are strongly absorbed by particulate matter, they reach river systems only under flood
conditions where soil particles are washed into the rivers, through evaporation, through codistillation with
water, and through wind-caused soil erosion. Estimates
of the proportion of the annual production of organochlorine pesticides reaching the sea have ranged from a high
of 90 percent to a more conservative 40-60 percent[37] (see
Tables 1.12, 1.13, and 1.14 for production figures).

TABLE 1.12

U.S. Production and Consumption of DDT

Year	Production	Consumption
1950	35	26
1952	45	32
1954	44	20
1956	63	30
1958	66	30
1960	75	37
1962	76	30
1964	56	23
1966	64	21
1968	63	15

Note: Total production, 1944-68 = 1,225,000 metric
tons. Ten-year production, 1959-68 = 676,000 metric tons.

    Once in the sea, these pesticides may be concentrated
either in surface slicks or by marine organisms. DDT, for
example, is known to be distributed on a world basis from
an analysis of marine and arctic animals. Chlorinated
hydrocarbons are not readily metabolized, but dissolve in
fat; even when metabolism takes place, the reaction products are usually chlorinated hydrocarbons. Pesticides are

31

particularly likely to be concentrated in any oily material, including fish oils, because of their lipophilic/hydrophobic character. Therefore, they are found in appreciable concentrations in many marine organisms, especially those of high lipid content high in the food chain. Oysters alone have been found to amplify small concentrations of DDT 70,000 times in one month.[38]

TABLE 1.13

U.S. Production and Consumption of Andrin-Toxaphene Group
(thousands of metric tons)

Year	Production	Consumption
1956	39	28
1958	45	36
1960	41	34
1962	48	37
1964	48	38
1966	59	39
1968	55	18

Note: Ten-year production total, 1959-68 = 493,000 metric tons. Group includes aldrin, chlordane, dieldrin, endrin heptachlor, strobane, toxaphene.

TABLE 1.14

U.S. Production of Synthetic Organic Pesticides
(thousands of metric tons)

Year	Production
1960	294
1962	332
1964	356
1966	457
1968	545
1969	505

Note: Ten-year production total, 1959-68 = 3.79 million metric tons. Group includes insecticides, fungicides, and herbicides.

TABLE 1.15

Magnification Factors of Five Selected Mollusks

Pesticide	Magnification Range
Lindane	10- 250
Endrin	500-1,250
Methoxychlor	300-1,500
Dieldrin	700-1,500
Heptachlor	250-2,500
Aldrin	350-4,500
DDT	1,200-9,000

Note: Mention of any trade name in this report does not constitute endorsement of the product by the federal government.

While certain organochlorides have been in use for the past thirty years, their precise mode of action is not fully understood. Most scientists agree that they disrupt the transmission of impulses to the central nervous system. Recently, sublethal effects on calcium deposition in birds' eggs have been recognized. They are, it is known, acutely toxic to many marine organisms in proper concentrations; concentrations in water as low as 0.003 parts per million (ppm) have been lethal to shrimp.

The following have been termed the major marine pollutants from the pesticide group:

1. Organochlorines. To date there is little evidence that human health has been directly affected by eating fish contaminated with organochlorine pesticide residues. Kills of fish and shellfish populations have been demonstrated in certain estuarine environments, particularly in the United States. One of the most serious kills was caused by the widespread application of insecticides to control fire ants in the southeastern part of the United States. The spraying programs were apparently initiated without consideration of the potential unsought consequences as the heavy toll of birds, fish, and other mammals was phenomenal.[39] One tidal study indicated that a tidal marsh treated with 0.2 pounds of DDT per acre would result in the death of 98 percent of the animals within three weeks of treatment.[40] Another demonstrated

that trophic magnification of DDT residues in the estuarine food web resulted in the reproductive failure of sea trout populations. Little is known about the chronic effects of the organochlorines on fish or other aquatic organisms.

2. <u>Polychlorinated biphenyl compounds</u>. PCBs have a wide range of industrial uses, the majority of which are in the electrical industry. They are not usually sprayed over wide areas except when used in association with a pesticide. The precise route of PCBs to the sea is unknown; loss from industrial use and sewage sludge contain some PCB that reaches the sea.

PCBs behave much the same way as organochlorine in persistency, accumulation, and distribution. They are as widely spread in the marine environment as DDT, and their persistence is greater. Their acute toxicity is generally lower, although there is some evidence that they have a high chronic toxicity. Like DDT they have been implicated in eggshell thinning in birds' eggs. There are few if any known incidents of ill effects on man that have been associated with the levels of PCB in marine products; illness and death have been reported in incidents of gross industrial exposure.[41]

3. <u>Organophosphates</u>. The organophosphate insecticides are also known as the anticholinesterase insecticides, the most widely written about pesticides not too long ago.[42] They have a unique capacity for poisoning (or inhibiting) cholinesterase, an enzyme essential to the orderly operation of the nervous system. The muscles of fish show a higher cholinesterase level than most mammalian muscles.

Organophosphates are relatively soluble in water and may be carried to rivers and the sea in substantial amounts as a result of land runoff. Most are less stable than the organochlorine types, and are therefore much less persistent in the environment. They are slowly hydrolyzed on contact with water and are much less hydrophilic. Bioaccumulation is comparatively unimportant. Because they are not persistent, they are found primarily in estuaries where their acute toxicity to marine animals is reasonably well documented. No cases of poisoning through the consumption of marine organisms contaminated with the substance have been reported or seem likely to occur. The danger they present is the large-scale destruction of new-born aquatic creatures in estuarine zones.

4. Carbamate compounds. These compounds, particularly carbaryl (Sevein), are now in fairly widespread use.

While the primary application is presently in agriculture, carbaryl is rapidly replacing DDT in malarial control programs. None of the compounds are particularly stable, nor have they been detected on a wide scale in sea waters or marine animals. They are mainly found in the silt of estuarine environments following local use on land and in mariculture (especially as a means of controlling crustacean pests in shellfish cultivation programs). Like the organophosphates, carbamates inhibit cholinesterase and other enzyme activities. Their toxicity follows a highly variable pattern. Carbaryl is moderately toxic to crustaceans but not to fish or mollusks. Harm to human health through eating contaminated fish or shellfish seems improbable.[43]

METALS

Heavy metal salts are soluble in water and stable in solution; they tend to persist for extended lengths of time. Many are highly toxic to marine organisms, which accumulate and concentrate them (see Table 1.16). The presence of small concentrations of certain metals can be deleterious to all kinds of life.[44] The primary sources of heavy metal contamination of the marine environment include agricultural use as pesticides, germicides, or fungicides; metal processing factories; and electrical, chemical, and pharmaceutical industries.

Mercury

Mercury is the most serious environmental contaminant among the heavy toxic metals; its deleterious effects are permanent. Absorbed and accumulated up through the food web, mercury has been known to poison fish, chicken, pigeons, storks, cattle, dogs, horses, rabbits, and man. The maximum permissible level of mercury for human food, including fish, has been set at 0.5 parts per million. Tuna and other fish have been removed from the U.S. market on various occasions by the Food and Drug Administration for exceeding these limits.

Various studies have indicated that mercury has toxic, teratogenic, and genetic effects on marine life and those who consume or feed on that life. The most disastrous large-scale poisoning occurred in Minamata, Kyushu, Japan, in the late 1950s, when 111 persons were poisoned as a result of eating fish or shellfish taken from Minimata Bay; 41 eventually died (see Figure 1.11).[45] Another outbreak occurred in Nigata City, Japan, with 26 cases and 5 deaths due to the same cause.[46] The mercury was traced to an effluent of waste mercury salt from industrial plants that used mercury chloride as a catalyzer in the production of vinyl chloride and acetaldehyde.

TABLE 1.16

Enrichment Factors for the Trace Element Composition of Shellfish Compared with the Marine Environment

	Enrichment Factors		
Element	Scallop	Oyster	Mussel
Ag	2,300	18,700	330
Cd	2,260,000	318,000	100,000
Cr	200,000	60,000	320,000
Cu	3,000	13,700	3,000
Fe	291,500	68,200	196,000
Mn	55,500	4,000	13,500
Mo	90	30	60
Ni	12,000	4,000	14,000
Pb	5,300	3,300	4,000
V	4,500	1,500	2,500
Zn	28,000	110,300	9,100

Source: Brooks and Rumsby (1965).

The annual production of mercury is approximately 9,000 tons, most of which is used by industry, especially the chloralkali groups. Theoretically no losses of mercury should occur, but in fact approximately 250 grams of mercury are lost per ton of chlorine produced.[47] Much of this finds its way into the marine environment via rivers or the atmosphere. Other uses of mercury include the manufacture of electrical switches, batteries, and the production of high-grade antifouling paints. Another large source is the burning of oils and coals that contain low concentrations that are carried out to sea in the atmosphere and dropped by rain. Because mercury is expensive, attempts have been made to recover and reuse it. In 1968, 46 percent of total world consumption was recycled.[48]

FIGURE 1.11

Production of Acetaldehyde at Minamata Factory
and Number of Cases of Minamata Disease, 1952-60

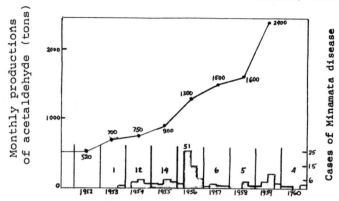

Source: K. Irukayama, The Pollution of Minamata Bay
and Minamata Disease, Advan. Water Pollution Research,
3:153-180, 1967.

A variety of organic mercurial compounds also are
used in agriculture and horticulture for the control of
seedborne and fungal diseases and in the paper industry
as slimicides. These compounds have low water solubility
and reach aquatic environments only under flood conditions. Such usages account for about one-half of the
world production; they have been held responsible for increases in the mercury content of birds collected in
Sweden, where the levels in the 1940s and 1950s were 10
to 20 times those from previous years.

Lead

The input of lead into the marine environment as a
result of man's activities is now in excess of the supply
from natural processes. The oceans of the northern hemisphere have been polluted to such a degree that industrial lead input has elevated average lead concentrations
by a factor of two or three. World production of this
toxic metal is approximately three million tons per year,
over 10 percent of which is used in leaded gasoline and

motor fuels where it functions as an antiknock agent.[49]
Over 2 x 10[5] tons of lead reach the marine environment
from this source alone.[50] An equal amount is introduced
in effluents from chemical factories and the natural
processes of weathering.

It is not exactly clear how industrial pollution
lead reaches the oceans via rivers. Sludge removal in
sewage treatment plants removes a large fraction of industrial lead in wastes (according to the U.S. Public
Health Service), but runoff of storm waters from paved
areas, buildings, and plant foliage in coastal cities
does not go through this process, contributing significant amounts. Present concentrations of industrial pollutants in rivers are so excessive that exchange between
particulate and dissolved forms is significant in providing large amounts of dissolved lead even though the major
fraction is absorbed onto solids. More than one-third of
lead production goes into automobile batteries, where it
can be recycled without excessive loss.[51] However, the
world's leading lead consumer (the United States) eventually recycles as scrap only 60 percent of the lead it
consumes.[52]

FIGURE 1.12

Profiles of Lead Concentrates
in Ocean Waters

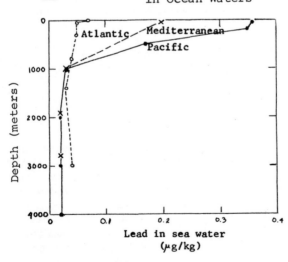

Atlantic (Bermuda,
32 10'N, 64 30'E);
Mediterranean (West
End, 40 39'N, 05
40'E); and Pacific
(California Coast
29 13'N, 117 37'W).

Source: Data from Chow and Patterson (1966).

Lead concentrates in the surface layers of near-shore sediments in greater quantities than in subsurface layers, persisting for long periods of time. Although (to this writer's knowledge) there have been no reports of human poisoning by eating marine products with high lead contamination, the rapid increase of lead levels in the marine environment must be viewed with concern. Lead is highly toxic. As there is no known threshold level for physiological damage, exposed organisms may be adversely affected. Lead accumulates in marine animals and can act as an enzyme inhibitor and/or impair cell metabolism. Acute exposure is likely to damage gill surfaces and inhibit oxygen-carbon dioxide transfer.

Other Metals

The large-scale production of copper and zinc (5 million tons), chromium (2 million tons), and cadmium poses potential hazards of marine pollution.[53] Copper and zinc are used in large quantities for water pipes and water storage tank plating, as plating and galvanizing is used to prevent rust. Quantities of copper and lead are found in measurable amounts in sewage sludges, particularly in industrial areas. Copper and zinc salts are used in a variety of industries. Copper is also used on a small scale in pesticide formulations. Plating and metallurgical industries use cadmium in electrolytic processes. Cadmium is also used as a pigment and a catalyst in some other industrial processes. In most cases, the route to the marine environment for all of these metals is via rivers and sewage or industrial outfall.

Toxicity levels for these metals are predictive, but certain interactions are antagonistic and synergistic--two factors of great importance in any biological consideration of water pollution. Biological effects are dependent on temperature, salinity, density, and the amounts of other metals in the immediate environment. Zinc and cadmium, for example, act additively to reduce their toxic effects, while zinc-nickel and zinc-copper combinations act synergistically, the latter combinations being five times as toxic as the anticipated combined effects. More data on single and combination effects are needed.

Many effects of cadmium toxicity have been demonstrated in animals, but only two have been demonstrated in man: decalcification and "itai-itai" found in Japan. One expert reports that anemia is one of the earliest

manifestations of cadmium toxicity among exposed industrial workers. As with lead, there appears to be no useful purpose for cadmium in man, and the potential for
harm is great.

DOMESTIC WASTE

Domestic waste includes domestic sewage, wastes from
food processing, detergents, runoff from agricultural
areas, and dredging spoils. When untreated, it has five
major polluting characteristics:
     1. A high bacterial content with parasites and pos-
sibly virus concentrations that contaminate mollusks and
shellfish and limit the use of bathing areas.
     2. Dissolved organic and suspended constituents
that place a high biochemical oxygen demand in decompo-
sition.
     3. High nutrient concentrations of phosphorus and
nitrogen compounds that enrich receiving waters and speed
eutrophication.
     4. Flotables of organic or inorganic constituents
that cause serious amenity problems and interfere with
primary production and self-purification processes.
     5. Bottom sludge with trace concentrations of heavy
metal contaminants.
     The bulk of pollution from wastes arises from the in-
tentional discharge of materials into rivers or from effluent points located on coasts; their effects are more
dependent on population and its distribution than any
other form of pollution.[54] A 1966 United Nations survey
cited domestic wastes as the single most important marine
pollution problem.[55] Agricultural practices, with fertilizers and domestic animal wastes, make one of the largest single contributions; in the United States, it has
been estimated that the volume of animal waste is ten
times as great as the volume of human waste (see Table
1.17).[56]
     Overfertilization and poisoning are two of the most
important effects of domestic waste. Overfertilization
becomes evident when marine populations of plant life increase very quickly, causing "blooms." Blooms of phyto-
plankton caused fish kills along the Florida Gulf coast
in 1916, 1932, 1948, 1952-54, and every year between 1957
and 1964. Although these blooms, known as the "red tide,"
are believed to occur naturally, they have become more
frequent with increased manmade nutrient disposal.

TABLE 1.17

Estimated Amounts and Costs of U.S. Wastes Barged to Sea, 1968

Wastes	Pacific Coast Disposal Tons	Pacific Coast Disposal Cost (dollars)	Atlantic Coast Disposal Tons	Atlantic Coast Disposal Cost (dollars)	Gulf Coast Disposal Tons	Gulf Coast Disposal Cost (dollars)
Dredging spoils	7,320,000	3,175,000	15,808,000[a]	8,608,000	15,300,000	3,800,000
Industrial wastes (chemicals, acids, caustics, cleaners, sludges, waste liquors, oily wastes, etc.):						
Bulk	981,000	991,000	3,011,000	5,406,000	690,000	1,592,000
Containerized	300	16,000	2,200	17,000	6,000	171,000
Garbage and trash[b]	26,000	392,000	--	--	--	--
Miscellaneous (airplane parts, spoiled food, confiscated material, etc.)	200	3,000	--	--	--	--
Sewage sludge	--	--	4,477,000[c]	4,433,000	--	--
Construction and demolition debris	--	--	574,000	430,000	--	--
Total	8,327,500	4,577,000	23,872,200	18,894,000	15,996,000	5,563,000

Note: Table does not include outdated munitions.

[a]Includes 200,000 tons of fly ash.

[b]At San Diego, dumping of 4,700 tons of vessel garbage was discontinued in November 1968.

[c]Tonnage on wet basis. Assuming average 4.5 percent dry solids, this amounts to approximately 200,000 tons per year of dry solids barged to sea.

Source: Dillingham Corporation, Marine Disposal of Solid Wastes (under contract to Department of Health, Education and Welfare, Bureau of Solid Wastes Management, October 1968).

Of the major nutrients (nitrogen, phosphorus, and potassium) man introduces into the marine environment, phosphorus can cause the most serious pollution problems. Phosphates enter the oceans from rivers and outfalls via sewage, where their origin is largely in the form of polyphosphate builders in detergent formulations. Agricultural runoff from fertilizers is the second source.[57] Nitrates reach the sea from fossil fuel burning and subsequent rainfall over the sea, and from runoff nitrate fertilizer usage on land.[58] Sewage effluents contain nitrate and ammonia nitrite, both of which are oxidized to nitrate by bacteria.

TABLE 1.18

Nutrient Budget of World's Oceans
(in millions of metric tons)

	Nitrogen	Phosphorus	Silicon
Reserve in ocean	920,000	120,000	4,000,000
Annual use by phyto-plankton	9,600	1,300	--
Annual contribution by rivers	19	14	4,300
Dissolved	19	2	150
Suspended	0	12	4,150
Annual contribution by rain	59	0	0
Annual loss to sediments	9	13	3,800

Source: Emery et al. (1955).

Nitrates and phosphates are essential nutrients in the productivity of the marine environment. But the over-abundance of these ions can lead to eutrophication of fresh water lakes and bodies, followed by deoxygenation and anaerobic decay. Eutrophication of lakes caused by phosphorus from domestic sewage, eroded soil, and farm manure is a serious problem in practically every country; it serves as a model of what may happen to estuaries and coastal oceans in the future. In fact, similar phenomena have already been recorded in certain marine fjord and estuarine environments.[59] While persistent, neither nitrate nor phosphorus causes toxic effects within marine

animals. Their primary impact is upon coastal zones in
the depletion of oxygen, a process that could have far-
reaching effects. Of commercially important fish, 90 percent reside, pass, or breed in estuaries. By the year
2000, over 20 percent of the world's animal protein may
come from the sea; therefore, the health of estuaries is
vital to mankind.

There is no reliable knowledge on the amount of phosphorus mined by man that eventually reaches the environment. Lack of production data makes even estimates difficult. However, areas heavily affected by sewer sludge
are known to be devoid of normal benthic communities.
These areas generally include the portions of the sewer
sludge and dredge spoil disposal areas in which dried
sediments contain more than 10 percent organic matter.[60]
The dumping of contaminated sludge from sewer operations
and dredge spoils in coastal waters off New York City
over a 40-year period has resulted in two separate impov-
erished areas of normal benthic fauna totaling over 20
square miles. Other dredging operations, although not
directly toxic to marine life, have been reported to lead
to increased turbidity and reduced primary productivity
in marine life. The fine material stirred up on dredging
operations affects the migration of fishes and often
drives them away.

MILITARY WASTE

The dumping of obsolete or dangerous military wastes
into the oceans has, until recently, been considered an
acceptable method of disposal by most members of the international community. Munitions dumping areas are designated on most nautical charts, and the times and hazards
posted in Notice to Mariners. These wastes have consisted
of organic materials, biological and chemical warfare
agents, heavy metals, petrochemicals, outdated explosives,
defoliating agents, pesticides, solid objects, dredging
spoils, and other inorganic materials peculiar to military establishments. Because of the classified aspect
of military operations, the exact chemical and toxicological nature of these materials is frequently unknown, and
details on the dumping of these materials are generally
not available.

The 1969-70 congressional investigations of the U.S.
Army's CHASE (cut holes and sink 'em) operations provided
one of the first full-scale reconsiderations of the

practice and resulted in a Defense Department policy change and a moratorium on all such disposal operations.[61] A study by the National Academy of Sciences revealed that alternatives did exist for the majority of the munitions the Army wished to dump, and that the possible hazards inherent in the sea disposal were too great to risk. However, 418 concrete containers of nerve gas rockets were eventually dumped, there being no acceptable demilitarization alternative. A follow-up sampling of water in the disposal area revealed no indication of gas leakage or immediate environmental damage.

Military operations also pollute the oceans in other ways. Nuclear submarines discharge contaminated resins and reactor cooling water on occasion. Naval vessels discharge oil and sewage in routine operation. Chemical defoliants used to destroy cover areas in Vietnam have found their way to the South China Sea, contaminating part of a significant fishery. On May 2, 1973, Japan's social and health ministry disclosed that it had impounded 24 tons of frozen shrimp from South Vietnam pending the outcome of tests.

NOTES

1. See, for example: Joint Group of Experts on the Scientific Aspects of Marine Pollution, Reports, Sessions 1-4; unpublished mimeo, Secretary of the Interior, The National Estuarine Pollution Study (Washington, D.C.: U.S. Government Printing Office, 1970); Oscar Schachter, Marine Pollution Problems and Remedies (New York: United Nations Institute for Training and Research, 1970); Mary M. Sibthorp, Oceanic Pollution: A Survey and Some Suggestions for Control (London: David Davies Memorial Institute of International Studies, June 1969).

2. GESAMP I/II, p. 5. Unpublished mimeo.

3. Charles E. Wilbur, The Biological Aspects of Water Pollution (Springfield, Ill.: C. C. Thomas, 1969), p. 82.

4. Schachter, op. cit., p. 7.

5. See Max Blumer, "Oil Pollution in the Oceans," in Hoult, ed., Oil on the Sea (New York: Plenum Press, 1969), p. 6, for method of estimate.

6. Joint Group of Experts on the Scientific Aspects of Marine Pollution, Report of the Third Session (Rome: FAO, February 1971), UN Doc GESAMP III/19, Annex IV; Luther J. Carter, "Global Environment: MIT Study Looks for Signs of Danger," Science, August 14, 1970.

7. Schachter, *op. cit.*, p. 8.

8. Some 25 percent of the world's oil production passes through the English Channel. See Blumer, *op. cit.*, p. 6.

9. *Hearings* before the U.S. Congress on the 1969 Brussels Conventions, Senate Committee on Public Works, Subcommittee on Environment, p. 195; Bruce Halstead, "Toxicological Aspects of Marine Pollution" (mimeo.).

10. Blumer, *op. cit.*

11. The 35-day BOD of anthracene is 1.18; cyclohexane 3.18. One mg. of various hydrocarbons requires 4 mg. of oxygen to completely oxidize. The values are obviously high when compared to BOD for glucose (1.07), protein (1.18), and vegetable and animal oil (2.9). See Claude E. Zobell, *Advances in Water Pollution* 3, no. 85 (1964): 109, for oxidation rates.

12. Schachter, *op. cit.*, p. 9.

13. Blumer, *op. cit.*, p. 7.

14. See U.S. Environmental Protection Agency, Water Quality Office, "Oil Pollution Implications, Platform 'Charlie' Main Pass Block 41 Field, Louisiana" (U.S. Government Printing Office, May 1971).

15. Halstead, *op. cit.*

16. See K. J. Whittle and M. Blumer, "Chemostasis in Starfish," in Hoult, ed., *op. cit.*, p. 13.

17. Blumer, *op. cit.*, p. 10.

18. George A. Duomani, *Science, Technology, and American Diplomacy: Exploiting the Resources of the Seabed* (Washington, D.C.: U.S. Government Printing Office, July 1971), p. 40.

19. *Ibid.*, p. 41.

20. U.S. Commission on Marine Science, Engineering and Resources, *Panel Reports*, Vol. 3 (Washington, D.C.: U.S. Government Printing Office, 1969), p. VII-193.

21. *Ibid.*

22. Robert W. Holcomb, "Oil in the Ecosystem," *Science*, October 10, 1969, p. 204.

23. Duomani, *op. cit.*, p. 41.

24. Rogers C. B. Morton, Television Interview with Senator Edward Brooke (Mass.), Sunday February 6, 1972.

25. Theodore Rice and D. A. Wolfe, "Radioactivity--Chemical and Biological Aspects," in Donald W. Hood, ed., *Impingement of Man on the Oceans* (New York: Wiley, 1971), p. 332.

26. National Academy of Sciences-National Research Council, *The Effects of Atomic Radiation on Oceanography and Fisheries*, Publication 551 (Washington, D.C., 1957), p. 6.

27. Rice and Wolfe, op. cit., p. 340.

28. Ibid.

29. Arnold B. Joseph, "United States's Sea Disposal Operations: A Summary to December 1956" (Oak Ridge, Tenn.: Technical Information Service, August 1957).

30. Ibid., p. 8.

31. Report by John W. Gofman and Arthur R. Tamplin cited in Barry Commoner, The Closing Circle (New York: Alfred A. Knopf, 1971), p. 62.

32. Ibid.

33. U.S. Council on Environmental Quality, Ocean Dumping: A National Policy (Washington, D.C.: U.S. Government Printing Office, October 1970).

34. The European Nuclear Energy-Organization for Economic Cooperation and Development (ENEA-OECD), Radioactive Waste Disposal Operations in the Atlantic, 1967 (Paris: OECD, September 1968).

35. See especially J. C. Headly, The Pesticide Problem: An Economic Approach to Public Policy (Baltimore: Johns Hopkins Press, 1967); R. W. Riseborough, "Chlorinated Hydrocarbons in Marine Ecosystems," in M. W. Miller, ed., Chemical Fallout (Springfield, Ill.: C. C. Thomas, 1969); Philip Butler, "Pesticides--A New Factor in Coastal Environments" (ed. by James B. Trefethen), Transactions of the 34th North American Wildlife and Natural Resources Conference (Washington, D.C.: Wildlife Management Institute, 1969).

36. GESAMP III/19, op. cit., Annex IV, p. 6.

37. Ibid.

38. National Estuarine Pollution Study, op. cit., p. 248.

39. Ibid., p. 280.

40. Wilbur, op. cit., p. 121.

41. GESAMP III/19, op. cit., p. 7.

42. Wilbur, op. cit., p. 95.

43. GESAMP III/19, op. cit., p. 9.

44. National Estuarine Pollution Study, op. cit., p. 245; Wilbur, op. cit., p. 60.

45. Massachusetts Institute of Technology, Study of Critical Environmental Problems (MIT Study) (Cambridge, Mass.: MIT Press, 1971), p. 137.

46. Ibid.

47. GESAMP III/19, op. cit., p. 13.

48. MIT Study, op. cit., p. 263.

49. GESAMP III/19, op. cit., p. 13.

50. Ibid.

51. Clair Patterson, "Lead," in Hood, ed., op. cit., pp. 245-59.

46

52. _Ibid._
53. Ron Eisler, "Cadmium Poisoning in Fundulus Heteroclitus," _Journal of Fisheries Research Board of Canada_ 28, no. 9 (1972).
54. Wilbur, _op. cit._, p. 140.
55. Schachter, _op. cit._, p. 54.
56. Wesley Marx, _The Frail Ocean_ (New York: Ballantine Books, 1969): Chapter 2 describes the case of Florida red tides in detail.
57. _MIT Study_, _op. cit._, p. 146.
58. _Ibid._, p. 148.
59. GESAMP III/19, _op. cit._, p. 11.
60. J. B. Pearce, "The Effects of Solid Waste Disposal on Benthic Communities in the New York Bight" (Rome: FAO, November 24, 1970).
61. See hearings before the Foreign Affairs Subcommittee on International Organizations and Movements of the U.S. House of Representatives, 91st Congress, 1st Session, May 8, 13, 14, 15, 1969: _International Implications of Dumping Poisonous Gas and Waste into Oceans_ (Washington, D.C.: U.S. Government Printing Office, 1969); hearings before the Commerce Subcommittee on Oceanography of the U.S. Senate, 91st Congress, 2nd Session, August 5, 1970: _Dumping of Nerve Gas Rockets in the Ocean_ (Washington, D.C.: U.S. Government Printing Office, 1970).

2

STATUS OF MARINE POLLUTION
IN INTERNATIONAL LAW

INTRODUCTORY NOTE: ABUSE OF RIGHTS

Attempts to limit abuse of rights are expressed in international law, which limits the rights of one state in order to safeguard the general interests of the international community. The general notion of freedom of the high seas has always contained an inherent danger of abuse, and indeed the international community has long since evolved rudimentary rules to insure that the high seas do not become a legal vacuum. The crime of piracy, for example, was early recognized jure gentium as one of universal jurisdiction, as freedom of the seas was recognized only to vessels flying a flag of a state under whose jurisdiction it might be recognized.[1]

The earliest uses of the ocean were easy to reconcile. Navigation and fishing, the main uses, were not incompatible. The amount of waste disposed in the sea was insignificant compared to its great size. Gradually, however, the uses of the sea increased and the regulation of conflicting uses became more and more essential.

The control of marine pollution has been a recognizable element of international law only since World War II. The language of law governing its control has been vague and general for most substances, relying primarily on the rule of reasonableness. Specific control provisions were adopted only for particular pollutants with high visibility and obvious hazard. Until recently, international law was directed almost exclusively at the problems of oil pollution from ships and radioactive substances from fallout and waste disposal. Where attempts have been made to cover all forms of marine pollution, they have resulted in convention provisions so broad as to appear more as recommendations than as a comprehensive basis for a system of control.

National legal systems cannot unilaterally regulate competing uses of the sea beyond their territorial and contiguous zone jurisdiction (three and twelve miles respectively) without running directly counter to the well-established principle of freedom of the seas. States have therefore relied on more and more international management and agreement for the control of pollution-causing activities outside these zones.

In this chapter the status of marine pollution control provisions in international law is examined chronologically. The progression reveals a philosophic evolution, a change in the attitude of an international community that increasingly recognizes the need for stronger and more comprehensive international controls. It also demonstrates the extent to which international law lags behind technological change and the enormity of the effort that will be required to make up the difference.

The international control of marine pollution proceeds at two levels: (1) in specific treaty and convention provisions directed toward specific pollutants and (2) in major areas of sea law that relate to pollution control in a more general jurisdictional sense. Thus, while continental shelf law is primarily designed to encourage offshore mineral exploitation, the manner of jurisdictional exercise is crucial to the quality of control of pollution arising from such activity. The analysis of the evolutionary direction of sea law shows profound implications for the future control of marine pollution.

HUGO GROTIUS

With the publication of Mare Liberum (Freedom of the Seas) in November 1608, Hugo Grotius, the "Father of International Law," established the doctrine of the freedom of the sea. "The sea," he said, "can in no way become the private property of any one, because nature not only allows but enjoins its common use."[2]

Despite the author's questionable objectivity--he was employed by the Dutch East India Company to refute the claims of Spain and Portugal to exclusive ownership of the high seas--the concept gained status in customary international law as nations came to recognize its mutual advantage. Even at the height of their seapower, the English adopted the principle. Queen Elizabeth I acknowledged that "The use of the sea and air is common to all. Neither can title to the oceans belong to any people or private persons, for as much as neither nature nor public use or custom permit any possession there of."[3]

In his arguments Grotius used two Latin phrases to describe the conflicting perspectives over sea law. The oceans, he demonstrated, have been considered both res nullis (belonging to no one) and res communis (belonging to everyone). Nation-states, he found, applied each concept to suit their circumstances; when possessed of strong navies, they operated under the former assumption; when weak, they invoked their privileges under the latter. Except in time of war, no nation sought to qualify freedom of the seas.

The advent of modern technology and the potential for deep sea mineral explitation have rendered Grotian high sea freedoms more and more obsolete.[4] To cope with these new possibilities, the international community commenced a redefinition of sea law to preserve old benefits in conjunction with new realities.

THE TRUMAN PROCLAMATION AND CONTINENTAL SHELF DOCTRINE

The Truman Proclamation of September 28, 1945, is generally regarded as the starting point in the redefinition of international sea law. Prior to that time it was widely accepted that all coastal states had some measure of authority over the resources of contiguous ocean floors, but that the area concerned was of minimal size. It was generally understood that the floor beneath internal waters and territorial sea was wholly within the disposition of the coastal state, and that no other state or national thereof could engage in exploitation of such resources without the consent of that state. Attempts to quarantine a 200-mile zone off the coast of the Americas to World War II belligerents were unenforceable. But the notion of an additional area of ocean bottom under "exclusive" coastal control emerged during World War II, and within a dozen years became widely accepted.[5]

Because of its legal status, economic significance, and potential for political and military conflict, the Truman Proclamation triggered a series of rapidly expanding and accelerating national claims to exclusive control

over the continental shelf (see Figures 2.1 and 2.2), defined in the proclamation as an "extension of the land
mass of the coastal nation and thus naturally pertinent
to it."[6] States adjacent to wide shelves with exploitable
resources followed suit. Many that refused or that had
no exploitable shelf staked compensatory claims to portions of the sea. Others merely expanded claims to larger
ocean areas.

FIGURE 2.1

Idealized Topographic Profile
of a Continental Margin

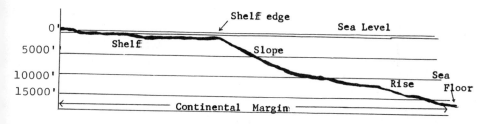

Source: "Petroleum Resources of the Continental Margins
of the United States," Exploiting the Ocean, T.W. Nelson and
C.A. Burk((Washington, D.C.: Marine Technology Society, 1966).

The rationale for the United States to claim jurisdiction over its shelf was based primarily upon its need
for new domestic sources of petroleum. By 1945 offshore
drilling operations were under way off Long Beach, California, and oil and sulfur resources had been detected in
the Gulf of Mexico off Louisiana and Texas. As a precau-
tionary step President Truman proclaimed exclusive U.S.
jurisdiction and control, but not sovereignty, over the
shelf resources. The President was careful to safeguard
the right of navigation in waters above the shelf--a
right the U.S. Navy could not afford to compromise. The
U.S. government reasoned that

> the exercise of jurisdiction over the natu-
> ral resources of the subsoil and sea bed of
> the continental shelf by the contiguous

FIGURE 2.2

Continental Shelves of the World

nation is reasonable and just, since the
effectiveness of measures to utilize and
conserve these resources would be contingent
upon cooperation and protection from the
shore.[7]

While the proclamation implicitly recognized the
lack of any internationally agreed guidelines for shelf
exploitation and the need for some form of regulation,
it explicitly provided a framework of national jurisdiction to assure offshore development. It also opened the
door for further unilateral extensions of jurisdiction
and sovereignty. By 1956 no less than 25 other states
had made similar claims to the shelf.[8]

THE INTERNATIONAL LAW COMMISSION AND
THE 1958 GENEVA CONVENTIONS

The confusion generated by the Truman Proclamation
made it evident that a new law of the sea would have to
be developed. The International Law Commission, a permanent organ of the United Nations, was entrusted with
the task of preparing a draft series of treaties for a
law of the sea conference as early as 1949. The succes-
sive drafts of the commission over 1950 to 1957 illus-
trate the relentless expansion of a once limited concept
of national jurisdiction. The development of the final
treaties, the Geneva Conventions of 1958, demonstrated,
as William T. Burke has said, "how far man's technological ingenuity and scientific ability exceed his political
foresight and the capacity to adapt his moral, political,
and legal conduct to the technological changes that have
revolutionized contemporary society."[9]

The operations and discussions of the commission are
important because of their impact on the 1958 Geneva Conference and the historical context they provide for future
sea law conferences.[10] In addition to redefining the
whole of sea law, the commission drafted treaties of specific and general relevance to the control of marine pollution. Specifically, the commission, and later the Geneva Conference, addressed itself to oil and nuclear
pollution. Coastal control of adjacent continental shelf,
access to contiguous zones, and width of territorial sea
resources were the primary elements having general relevance for control.

Between the 1945 Truman Proclamation and the 1956 final recommendations of the International Law Commission the majority of states making claim to areas of continental shelf refrained from stating any definition or delimitation of exclusive control by failing to define "continental shelf" in their national legislation. Chile, Costa Rica, and Korea laid claim to the shelf at "whatever depth" it might occur; Peru and Honduras "to whatever extent it might be"; and El Salvador to the shelf incidental to its exclusive control claim over an ocean zone off its coast 200 miles wide.[11] For practical purposes, however, most sought to delimit exclusive control within the 100-fathom or 200-meter isobath.

Discussions in the International Law Commission concerning the continental shelf definition, which began in 1950, seemed most affected by four factors:

1. A general belief that the major goal was to encourage resource exploitation in contiguous submarine areas.

2. The desirability of providing a clear definition to avoid future disputes.

3. The fear of states with little or no shelf that a depth-only definition would be prejudicial.

4. The fact that some areas already being exploited, particularly in the Persian Gulf, did not seem to be continental shelves at all.[12]

A 1951 commission draft article adopted a definition for continental shelf that was to complicate and impede the development of any international control for marine pollution protection or any other purpose. According to Article I of the draft, nation-states would assume jurisdiction over the seabed and subsoil of the submarine areas contiguous to their coasts, but outside the areas of their territorial waters, where the depth of the subjacent waters admits of the exploitation of the natural resources of the seabed and subsoil.

At the opening of the 1951 session the rapporteur, J. P. François, recommended that the continental shelf be definitively defined within a 100-fathom (200-meter) depth limit. Such a definition, he noted, would avoid the need to make specific mention of shallow water areas, would avoid reference to geological and geographic definitions of the continental shelf, and would give precision to the granted right by providing a fixed outer limit for it.[13] However, proponents of a more general definition prevailed.

By 1958 the International Law Commission had adopted the same exploitability criterion in Article 67 of its final draft as had been previously incorporated in Article 1 of the 1951 draft. Many delegates, particularly Garcia Amador of Cuba, supported the exploitability criterion in the interest of obtaining exclusive coastal state rights. Mr. Amador argued that even in setting a 200-meter limit in 1953 the commission had recognized that exclusive coastal rights did not depend on the existence of a continental shelf and that some other means must be found to provide non-shelf coastal states with some means of exercising control. Judging from the commentary on Article 67, however, it would appear that the commission believed that by providing a 200-meter limit on exclusive coastal rights it would actually prohibit future exploitation beyond that limit when it became possible.

Coastal state jurisdiction over adjacent seabed resources became customary international law when the Convention on the Continental Shelf of the 1958 Geneva Conference came into force on June 10, 1964. Responsibility for leasing, supervising, and controlling exploitation activities, although not specifically mentioned, was placed under the coastal state's jurisdiction and control. Pollution control measures for any offshore oil operations were de facto left to the coastal state's discretion through its own national laws.

Contemporary critics of the exploitability criterion expressed concern over the continuing uncertainty about the precise extent of offshore claims. Many feared the phenomenon of "creeping jurisdiction" in which "control and supervision" would gradually extend over not only the shelf, but also the waters above.[14] Others noted that

> a coastal state's rights over its shelf
> exist irrespective of any actual activity
> or occupation. Hence every coastal state
> would seem entitled to assert rights off
> its shores out to the maximum depth for
> exploitation reached anywhere in the world,
> regardless of its own capabilities or of
> local conditions, other than depth, which
> might prevent exploitation.[15]

Assuming the unlimited potential of technological progress, the criterion could lead to the hypothetical division of the sea floor shown in Figure 2.3.

FIGURE 2.3

Hypothetical Division of Sea Floor
Assuming Unlimited Progress in Exploitation Techniques

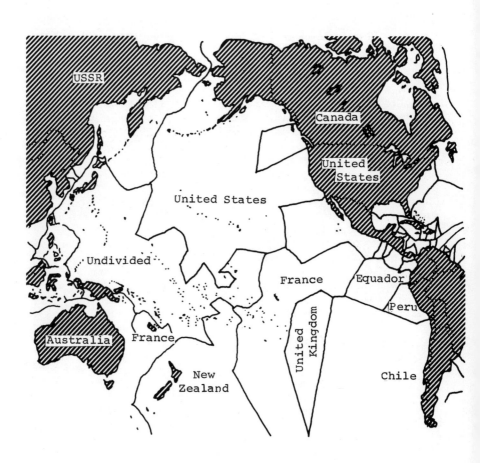

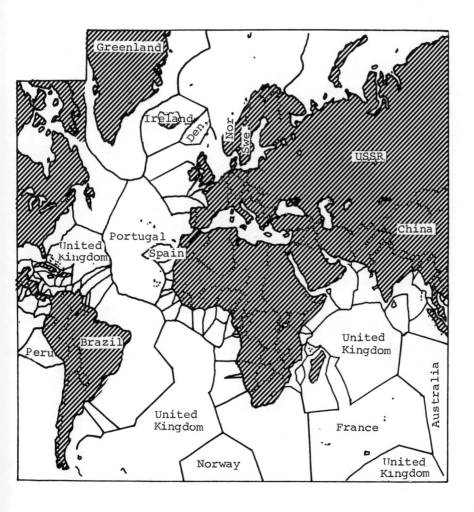

Supporters of the convention drew attention to the great weight attached to the "adjacent" requirement. In their judgment it was not their "intention to establish a horizontal instead of a vertical limit for the submarine areas--an entirely new concept completely foreign to those previously adopted by the Commission.[16] Others accurately noted that the degree of vagueness in the exploitability criterion, deplored by all commentators, seemed nevertheless

> much less likely to produce consequential
> tension than would a criterion which,
> while certain and precise, would also limit
> coastal authority to only part of an ex-
> ploitable area and perhaps permit com-
> pletely free and uncontrolled access by
> others to areas beyond coastal control but
> still of particular concern to the coastal
> state.[17]

Until 1962 sea law experts advocated the maintenance of the flexibility exploitability criterion until developing countries clarified their economic, political, and social goals. Without these goals the limits best designed to promote the common interests of all would be indiscernible.

Contiguous Zones

Part II, Article 24, of the 1958 Geneva Convention on the Territorial Sea and Contiguous Zone authorizes a coastal state, in a zone contiguous to its territorial sea but extending no farther than twelve miles from the baseline from which the breadth of the territorial sea is measured, to:

> Prevent infringement of its customs,
> fiscal, immigration, or sanitary regula-
> tions within its territory or territorial
> sea.
> Punish infringement of the above reg-
> ulations within its territory or territorial
> sea.[18]

The convention formally legitimized a pattern of mutual claim and, in most cases, reciprocal tolerance of certain exercises of unilateral control over access to a zone outside the normally accepted three-mile territorial water limit. Coastal states historically claimed control over access to these waters for many reasons--military security, fishing, mineral exploitation, customs inspection--and for the most part other states refrained from protesting these claims unless they appeared unreasonable.[19] On occasion states also have claimed a limited special authority for protection of "well-being," as in the projection of health, sanitation, and pollution regulations.[20]

As in the continental shelf dispute, the question of sovereignty versus jurisdictional control was raised in the 1958 Geneva Conference. The conference failed to define the competence to prescribe the extension of coastal state laws to the contiguous zone. States accepting the convention therefore have no obligation to repeal any national legislation, such as customs and security protection, that explicitly prescribes the regulation of activities upon the high seas.[21] The operating principle allowed, or more probably tolerated, that

> the coastal state should exercise certain
> limited powers of control in the contigu-
> ous zone in order to enable it to prevent
> eventual infringement within its terri-
> torial waters or territory of certain of
> its laws.[22]

The reasonableness criterion and the definition of "sanitary regulations" are tested in the Canadian Arctic Waters Pollution Prevention Act, described later in this chapter. Definitions of contiguous zone have been stretched under limited and strictly defined conditions in the International Maritime Consultative Organization Oil Pollution Conventions, also discussed later in this chapter. Whether coastal states may unilaterally legislate and enforce national antipollution laws outside the internationally recognized limits of their territorial waters remains an open question, despite the Contiguous Zone Convention.

High Seas

Pollution prevention and control on the high seas is a relatively new and complex part of international law. In the case of one pollutant, radioactive contamination

59

from fallout and waste, past efforts to arrive at control consensus were clouded by overriding national security-military political problems. In 1946 the United States unilaterally marked off large "danger zones" in the Pacific Ocean and warned maritime traffice of the potential hazards of radioactive fallout in those areas. A few years later both the United States and the USSR designated large ocean areas for missile and rocket testing. By 1955 the International Law Commission began its first serious effort to formulate a general doctrine of freedom of the seas for submission to the 1958 Geneva Conference.

To provide a basis for discussion on the issue of permissible uses of the sea at the commission's seventh session, J. P. François drew upon the conclusions of writers examining the use of the oceans for nuclear weapons testing[23] and recommended a "statement of principle" for the commission's consideration:

> The freedom of the high seas does not
> include the right to utilize the high seas
> in a manner which unreasonably prevents
> other states from enjoying that freedom.
> Scientific research and tests of atomic
> weapons on the high seas are only permitted
> subject to this qualification.[24]

At the eighth session one commission member expressed the view that the issue was whether a particular kind of use was permissible at all and, if so, to what extent.[25] Other delegates took the position that some uses of the sea, atomic testing in particular, were not permissible regardless of their reasonableness in terms of effects on other uses, and that whether they unreasonably interfered with use by other states was irrelevant.[26] Opponents of absolute prohibitions on certain uses (understood in this context to be atomic weapons testing) envisaged limitations based only on the reasonableness of the interference with other users. They argued that particular uses could not be considered impermissible a priori without regard for their effects on other uses.[27]

The commission made no expressed mention of controlling weapons testing in its final report. It did, however, state in the comment that the principle enunciated in paragraph 1, sentence 3, of the draft was applicable to weapons testing. According to that principle, "States are bound to refrain from any acts which might adversely affect the use of the high seas by nationals of other States."[28]

The 1958 Geneva Conference provided free access to the seas contingent upon accommodations in accord with the standard of reasonableness. Article 2 of the Convention on the High Seas specifically provided that freedom of the high seas "shall be exercised by all States with reasonable regard to the interests of other States in their exercise of the freedom of the high seas."[29] The convention codified a general principle of international law but created no implementing machinery to enforce the standard of reasonableness.

The Soviet Union was unable to persuade the 1958 conference to rule against weapons testing on the high seas,[30] and its ally, Poland, was unsuccessful in its attempt to elevate the third sentence of the commission's comment (see above) to the main treaty.[31] However, the conference did adopt an Indian resolution which warned "that there is a serious and genuine apprehension on the part of many states that nuclear explosions constitute an infringement of the freedom of the seas" and referred the problem to the United Nations General Assembly for appropriate action.[32]

RADIOACTIVE POLLUTANTS FROM WASTE DISPOSAL AND FALLOUT

The problem of radioactive pollution in the oceans did not end with the signing of the 1963 Nuclear Test Ban Treaty, which specifically forbids testing in ocean areas. Two nonsignatories, France and the People's Republic of China, continued to test nuclear weapons in an open-air manner that allows fallout to reach the sea. More dangerous, however, is that the oceans continue to be a depository for potentially harmful radioactive substances, and that this use may increase in the future.

Two basic philosophies govern all international discussions of radioactive waste disposal. The first is that such disposal is a legitimate, lawful use of the oceans provided that precautions, dictated by the substance and gaps in existing scientific knowledge, are observed. The second argues that radioactive contamination of the oceans is a violation of freedom of the seas, and therefore an impermissible use regardless of the safeguards adopted. Bridging both principles is the universal recognition that while individual states may now or eventually be able to formulate disposal programs incorporating "reasonable" scientific coastal safeguards, the fact remains that the ocean is a global phenomenon used by and affecting all states of the world; therefore, the cumulative impact of individually conceived programs devised without regard to those of other states and without cooperative efforts could conceivably endanger future safe uses of the oceans.[33]

Apart from Soviet insistence that no radioactive waste should be dumped into the ocean, there has been only one instance of international protest against a specific disposal practice. The government of Mexico protested a proposed disposal 180 miles south of Galveston and 150 miles east of Port Isabel, Texas, in the Gulf of Mexico. Despite the judgment of experts within the U.S. Atomic Energy Commission that the disposal would be "safe," the U.S. State Department and AEC staff ultimately recommended that the particular disposal not be authorized, and no new licenses were issued for sea disposal in the United States.[34]

Consistent concern for this problem on an intergovernmental level can be dated from 1956 in discussion of the International Law Commission. Because of the entanglement with the highly emotional problem of weapons testing, it was with difficulty that the commission was able to consider the disposal problem separately. One proposal, sponsored by Radhabinod Pal of India, would have prohibited any act that could not be managed in a way "to avoid any possible danger."[35] Opponents of weapons testing supported Pal's proposal, which was defeated only by a tie vote.

A more moderate provision, Article 48, which places states under an obligation to take steps to prevent pollution from radioactive waste disposal, was finally adopted without a dissenting vote. Paragraph 2 reads: "All States shall draw up regulations to prevent pollution of the seas from the dumping of radioactive waste."[36]

On the matter of weapons testing the commission blandly recommended in Article 48, paragraph 3, that: "All states shall co-operate in drawing up regulations with a view to the prevention of pollution of the seas or air space above, resulting from experiments or activities with radioactive materials or other harmful acts."[37] The attached comment made clear that the "many-sidedness of the subject" worked against it being amenable to the kind of general prohibition on radioactive waste disposal the commission thought it was recommending.[38]

Article 48, paragraph 2, of the commission draft was "meaningless for solving pollution problems because neither 'pollution' nor 'radioactive waste' was defined," according to a U.S. government study.[39] However, its potential impact was regarded with disquiet by states actually engaged in waste disposal operations.[40] Both the United States and the United Kingdom made efforts to delete paragraphs

2 and 3 at the 1958 Conference, ostensibly on the grounds
that Article 48 called for action by individual states and
"might lead to a lack of coordination, duplication of effort, and delay in finding an [international] solution."[41]
The Soviet bloc and other states also regarded the article
as inadequate, but for different reasons. They continued
in their efforts to prohibit all ocean disposal of radioactive waste. The resolution to delete paragraphs 2 and 3
passed the drafting committee by one vote, but the paragraphs were later restored to assure passage of the more
general provisions in plenary session.

Draft Article 48 became Article 25 of the Geneva Convention on the High Seas requiring signatory states to:

> Take measures to prevent pollution of
> the seas from the dumping of radioactive
> waste, taking into account any standards
> and regulations which may be formulated
> by the competent international organiza-
> tions. . . .
> Cooperate with the competent interna-
> tional organizations in taking measures
> for the prevention of pollution of the
> seas or air space above, resulting from
> any activities with radioactive materials
> or other harmful agents.[42]

The 1958 Conference further adopted a resolution recommending that the International Atomic Energy Agency (IAEA)
draw up internationally acceptable regulations to prevent
pollution of the sea by materials in amounts that would
adversely affect man and his marine resources.[43]

Following the conference, the IAEA convened a series
of panels, one of which dealt with the legal implications
of the disposal of radioactive waste into the sea (1963).
This panel produced two different drafts of a report re-
flecting the two divergent views on the permissibility of
disposing radioactive waste into the sea under general
principles of international law.[44] As a consequence, the
IAEA was not able to produce any "internally acceptable"
regulations to prevent pollution of the sea.

OIL POLLUTION

Although first the United States and then the League
of Nations undertook to foster explicit agreement upon

oil pollution control measures in the decade after World War I, nothing concrete was achieved until 1954 when the International Convention for the Prevention of Pollution of the Sea by Oil was concluded following an international conference. To date the oil convention is the only existing international agreement dealing exclusively with the prevention and control of marine pollution.[45]

The International Law Commission was able to make only modest recommendations, providing in Article 48, paragraph 1, that: "Every state shall draw up regulations to prevent pollution of the sea by the discharge of oil from ships or pipelines or resulting from the exploitation of the seabed and its subsoil, taking into account of existing treaty provisions on the subject."[46] The United States sought deletion of this provision at the 1958 Geneva Conference on the Law of the Sea. The U.S. representative argued that "it would be unwise to consider subjects already under study by the United Nations and specialized agencies"[47] and urged passage of a resolution recommending that all possible assistance be given to organizations studying the problem and that national programs designed to minimize the possibility of the pollution of the sea by oil be adopted. The United States later withdrew its resolution with the understanding that Article 48, paragraph 1, did in fact encourage each government to adopt definite programs to minimize oil pollution. The 1958 Geneva Conference adopted the International Law Commission article into Article 24 of the Convention on the High Seas, further requiring that "exploration" as well as exploitation be covered by the national regulations.

For fifteen years the 1954 London Convention remained the focal point but an incomplete answer for the problem of high seas oil pollution. By 1970 a total of 42 countries, including the major maritime nations, had signed the convention. Although these states owned more than two-thirds of total world shipping tonnage, they controlled rather less (about 60 percent) of world tanker tonnage.[48]

The 1954 Convention, as amended in 1962, prohibited the discharge of oil or an oily mixture of 100 parts per million within certain prohibited zones.[49] Naval vessels, ships employed by governments for noncommercial purposes, vessels under 500 gross tons, tankers under 150 tons, whaling vessels, and vessels on the Great Lakes were exempted from these regulations. Every ship to which the convention applies was required to carry an oil record book in which oil gains and losses were to be recorded.[50] The convention and its amendments entered into force on June 27, 1967.

Article VI provided that any contraventions of the agreement "shall be punishable under the law of the relevant territory in respect of the ships."[51] While the same article specifies that penalties "shall be adequate in severity to discourage any such unlawful discharge and shall not be less than the penalties which may be imposed under the law of that territory in respect of the same infringements within the territorial sea," no enforcement provisions were provided for vessels that fly "flags of convenience"[52] and which seldom visit their home ports where legal action could be taken. According to U.S. observers, "These vessels would appear to be immune, for all practical purposes, from the Convention."[53]

The 1967 Torrey Canyon disaster spurred the International Maritime Consultative Organization (IMCO) to consider further amendments to the Convention. In October 1969, the sixth IMCO Assembly approved further extensive amendments to the convention and its annexes which, apart from certain "practical" exemptions, are based on the principle of total prohibition of oil discharge.[54] The restrictions to be applied include:

1. Limitation of the total quantity of oil which a tanker may discharge in any ballast voyage to 1/15,000 of the total cargo carrying capacity of the vessel.
2. Limitation of the rate at which oil may be discharged to a maximum of 60 liters per mile traveled by the ship, and
3. Prohibition of discharge of any oil whatsoever from the cargo spaces of a tanker within 50 miles of the nearest land.[55]

The IMCO Assembly also approved a new form of oil record book to facilitate inspection. The 1969 amendments also included new provisions obliging governments receiving complaints of alleged contraventions to inform both IMCO and the reporting government of the action taken as a consequence of the information communicated.

THE BRUSSELS CONVENTIONS

The 1962 and 1969 amendments to the 1954 London Convention on Oil Pollution were deficient in a number of respects. Article III, while slightly modified, still exempted the following from the convention's control provisions:

1. The discharge of oil from a ship for the purpose of securing safety of a ship, preventing damage to a ship or cargo, or saving life at sea.
2. The escape of oil resulting from damage to a ship or unavoidable leakage, if all reasonable precautions following the damage were taken to prevent or minimize the escape.
3. The discharge of residue from oil discharged from fuel or lubricating oil purification.[56]

The 1967 Torrey Canyon disaster demonstrated the inadequacies of the convention as amended. The accident spurred IMCO to establish a legal committee to study the legal problems arising out of marine pollution. Following the work of this committee, IMCO convened an international legal conference in Brussels on November 10-28, 1969. The conference adopted and opened for signature two international conventions, one on intervention on the high seas in cases of oil pollution and the other on civil liability for oil pollution damages. These conventions were accompanied by three resolutions, one on international cooperation concerning pollutants other than oil, another on establishing an international compensation fund for oil production damage, and a third on the report of the working group on the fund.

Intervention on the High Seas in Cases of Oil Pollution

The first convention on intervention (known as the Public Law Convention) "constitutes a revolutionary departure from traditional concepts of the freedom of the high seas," according to Gerald Moore.[57] Article I of this convention provides that:

Parties to the . . . Convention may take such measures on the high seas as may be necessary to prevent, mitigate, or eliminate grave and imminent danger to their

coastline or related interest from pollution or threat of pollution of the sea by
oil, <u>following upon a maritime casualty</u>
<u>or acts related</u> to such a casualty which
may reasonably be expected to result in
major harmful consequences [emphasis
added].[58]

However, no measures are permitted against warships or
noncommercial ships owned or operated by a state. "Related interests" were defined as including: maritime, port,
or estuarine activities, including fishing; tourist at-
tractions; the health of a coastal population and the
well-being of the area concerned, including the conservation of living marine resources and wildlife.[59] Under
ordinary circumstances the acting coastal state must no-
tify the flag state and interested parties of the measures
it plans to take. Although under all circumstances the
measures must be proportionate to the anticipated damage
and must not exceed what is reasonable and necessary to
achieve the purposes of Article I (see above), in cases
of extreme urgency states may act without prior notifica-
tion or consultation.[60] Provision is made for the settle-
ment of disputes through a conciliation commission, composed of the two parties and an agreed-upon third party.
Appeals of this commission may be placed before an arbitration tribunal, similarly composed, whose judgments are
final.

Civil Liability for Oil Pollution Damages

The second Brussels convention (known as the Private
Law Convention) provides that the "owner of a ship at the
time of any occurrence, or series of occurrences having
the same origin, which causes pollution damage, shall be
liable for any pollution damage caused by oil."[61] However, <u>no</u> liability may be attached to the owner for pollution damage if he can prove that the damage resulted from
an act of hostility or natural phenomena of an excep-
tional, inevitable, and irresistible character or was
wholly caused by the negligence or omission or act of a
third party. Further, if the incident does not occur as
a result of the actual fault or privity of the ship's
owner, he may <u>limit</u> his liability under the convention in
respect to any one incident by an aggregate amount of
$100 U.S. per ton, but not to exceed $14 million.[62]

Enforcement of the convention is left to the contracting states; each contracting state is required to ensure that its courts possess the necessary jurisdiction to entertain actions for compensation. The convention also requires owners to maintain insurance or other financial security; the requirement is intended to promote improvements in ship equipment and design as a consequence of conditions that are likely to be required for insurance.[63]

ANALYSIS OF THE PRESENT FRAMEWORK OF INTERNATIONAL LAW GOVERNING MARINE POLLUTION CONTROL

Contemporary analyses of the existing framework of international law for the control of marine pollution unanimously agree that the present system is dangerously inadequate and that new law must be developed.[64] The trends and quantities of pollutants now entering the marine environment and the unilateral actions of certain states for pollution control purposes underline the need for change in the existing law and for the establishment of new treaties governing other substances. To justify this need, the emphasis of this analysis lies on the negative aspects of existing law.

Radioactive Substances

At present, "there is no effective international regulation of the disposal of radioactive waste into the sea," and "there is no international agreement on the conditions under which radioactive waste may be safely deposited into the sea."[65] No central international register records the nature, amount, or site of radioactive waste being dumped or released into the sea. And no international agency has been assigned the responsibility for surveying and monitoring the extent of the presence of radioactive isotopes in the oceans or in marine products. Two general provisions in the Convention on the Territorial Sea and the Contiguous Zone and in Article 25 of the Convention of the High Seas do not enhance environmental quality. Coastal states may unilaterally prohibit radioactive waste disposal in contiguous zones, but historically other states have not attempted disposal operations within a coastal state's 12-mile limit. Article 25 encourages states to cooperate in the handling of nuclear pollution problems but binds them to no particular method.

No protection is provided against the cumulative global impact of "safe" disposals within national territorial waters. And no state must follow waste disposal procedure codes established by the International Atomic Energy Agency, unless IAEA is the sole source of its fissionable materials or installations.[66]

Accidental releases of radioactive substances from nuclear vessels are covered by the 1962 Brussels Convention on the Liability of Operators of Nuclear Ships. This convention provides for civil liability, before municipal courts, of operators on a basis of absolute liability, subject to a limit of $300 million (U.S.) in respect to any one nuclear incident.[67] However, the convention does not concern itself with questions of state responsibility under international law. International claims may be removed if and only if they can be met under the municipal remedies of a contracting party pursuant to the convention. For the present, it has been the practice of a state anticipating a visit from the nuclear warships of another state to secure an indemnity against damage in advance of the visit.[68]

Nuclear weapons testing continues to contribute significant amounts of oceanic pollution despite the 1963 Nuclear Test Ban Treaty. France and the People's Republic of China did not sign the 1963 Test Ban Treaty. The practice of atmospheric testing has been, and continues to be, defended on the grounds that it is a unique problem that must be balanced between exclusive and inclusive use of the high sea and is ultimately dependent on the criterion of reasonableness. Applied to a state's recognized interest in protecting its own security, the claim is "in substance a claim to self-defense."[69] It is similar to such other exclusive use claims of areas of the high seas as security zones, missile testing, radar platforms, and the continental shelf. In such cases, "unlawfulness" would stem from the causing of injury to other states and their nationals to a degree that outweighs any reasonable assessment of the value to the testing state in protecting its own interests in security."[70]

Oil

International conventions governing the pollution of the sea by oil were the first international agreements for any marine pollutant. However, they have suffered from several severe deficiencies. Article VIII of the

1954 Oil Pollution Convention as amended (1962) requires
each state party to establish oil loading terminals in
every oil receiving port for the reception of waste oil
residues and oily mixtures. Several states, notably the
United States, have not adhered to this article. The
United States regards the provision of waste oil facilities on shore as the business of local municipalities,
port authorities, oil terminals, and private contractors.
Even though U.S. waste oil disposal standards are generally regarded as well above the world standard, the U.S.
National Committee for the Prevention of Pollution of the
Sea by Oil reasoned:

> If a foreign vessel were detected discharg-
> ing oily wastes off the U.S. coast (beyond
> the three-mile limit), and the government
> whose flag the ship flies sought to penalize
> the vessel as the result of a report from
> the United States, the shipowner might de-
> fend himself on the ground that the ship was
> bound for a U.S. port at which no facility
> existed. In that event the country of regis-
> try presumably would report the ship's state-
> ment to the United States authorities making
> reference to Article VIII, placing the United
> States in an embarrassing position if in fact
> no "adequate facility existed in that port."[71]

Without such facilities tanker captains have little
choice but to release oil in ballasting and tank cleaning
operations. Large quantities of oil released in these
operations can be avoided by universal adoption of the
"load-on-top" system.[72] Approximately 80 percent of the
world's tanker fleet employs this system. Pollution prevention, however, depends upon the effectiveness of oil-
water separators on board ship. And it is difficult to
obtain efficient separators, suitable for marine service,
for oil and water mixtures with essentially the same specific gravity.[73] Furthermore, waste oil facilities are
expensive to construct; opposition to mandatory installation is due to cost. The price of constructing and operating holding tanks ashore and on board tanker vessels to
eliminate discharges of oil ballast into the ocean has
been estimated by the American Institute of Merchant
Shippers as follows:

Facility	Cost
Worldwide capital investment required to provide ballast handling and treating facilities ashore	$1,600,000,000
Annual incremental operating costs for above	255,000,000
Worldwide capital costs of providing totally segregated ballast tanks to the extent that this is possible between now and 1980	2,700,000,000
Annual incremental operating costs for above	6,000,000[74]

However, such estimates ignore the profitability of recovery.

Enforcement and exceptions are two environmentally deficient provisions of the oil pollution convention. In the absence of uniform penalties for all states registering tanker fleets, many vessels violating the convention are able to avoid punishment. Vessels flying flags of convenience seldom visit their "home" ports where action could be taken, so for all practical purposes they are immune from the convention.[75] During one 18-month period ending in April 1957, for example, 31 foreign vessels of thirteen countries were found by the U.S. Coast Guard to have caused oil pollution.[76] Although many were chartered by American-owned oil companies, only three of the thirteen countries had laws under which their vessels could be penalized.

To alleviate this problem it has been suggested that the convention be modified to state that the penalties assessed against violators would be those of the country affected by the violation rather than those of the vessel's country of registry.[77] It has been further suggested that the crucial definition of "oil mixture" be upgraded to make enforcement practical. Under the convention's formula the strength of the oil mixture could not be proved without samples.[78] Moreover, the mixture described in Article I of the convention is unlikely in itself to cause marine life irreparable harm or to pollute beaches for very long; but the cumulative effects over the long term leading to higher concentrations and accumulations can. Sampling is both impractical and prohibitively expensive. Many argue that good faith that tanker masters will abide by the convention is a poor substitute for international regulation.

Exempting tankers under 150 tons and other ships under 500 tons in addition to naval ships and their auxiliaries is another weakness of the convention. The arguments used to justify such exemptions center around (1) the lack of administrative machinery to enforce regulation on the part of some states and (2) the sovereignty of warships. Most receiving ports, however, are located in highly developed countries with the necessary naval capacity to survey tanker traffic. Flag state enforcement of the convention for naval vessels would insure compliance and preserve military security. U.S. naval policy instructs all fleet components to observe the convention's enabling legislation in the United States, under the Oil Pollution Act of 1961.[79] There is no good reason why other states should not agree to do the same.

Article IV exempts liability if the escape of oil results from damage to a ship or unavoidable leakage. This clause limited Torrey Canyon liability since the owners claimed its protection. To partially alleviate the problem, the Brussels conventions specified liability provisions, but liability may still be limited if a shipowner can disprove "actual fault or privity." Due to this technicality the conclusions of the Liberian Board of Investigation could not have been more welcome to the Torrey Canyon owners. By ruling the ship's captain at fault, the board in effect absolved the owners of responsibility and reduced their liability.

Clearly some form of "no fault" insurance against environmental damage is needed that does not limit liability by subsidizing risk through the convention. Several conservation organizations, notably the Sierra Club in the United States, have declared their support for the principle of unlimited absolute liability for oil pollution damage, claiming that "the costs of unavoidable accidents, however caused, should be borne directly by the enterprise and not by individuals or governments suffering oil pollution damage."[80]

If the 1969 amendments to the 1954 Convention are adopted, a general ban on deliberate discharges to all areas of the sea would go into effect. But, like the convention they amend, the provisions allow several "practical" exceptions. It has been estimated that the formula proposed in Article III for allowable releases would permit nearly 550,000 barrels of oil to be dumped annually, a quantity that would increase proportionately with oil demand and increased tanker traffic.[81]

The 1969 Amendments to the 1954 Convention for the Prevention of Pollution of the Sea by Oil were designed to reduce the total amount of oil being discharged into the sea. Of the total 1.1 billion tons of oil that were shipped by sea in 1970, the following estimated amounts of cargo oil could have been legally released under the criteria of the 1954 Convention:

> 100 ppm criterion--59,000 long tons
> 60 liters per mile criterion--1,750,000
> long tons[82]

The language of the 1954 Convention would also permit a tanker to anchor a few miles off any coast and discharge its entire cargo as long as the discharge was at a rate of less than 100 parts per million.

Universal adoption of the 1969 Amendments would have restricted the total 1970 global oil discharge to approximately 73,000 long tons, as opposed to the estimated 550,000 long tons that were actually released, by limiting the rate of enroute tanker discharge to 60 liters per mile, not to exceed an absolute limit of 1/15,000 of its total cargo carrying capacity. The discharge limit based on a fraction of total cargo carrying capacity reduces the total amount of oil discharged into the sea at existing shipment levels. The total discharge will increase annually and proportionately with tanker size, tanker traffic, and oil demand.

In submitting the 1969 amendments to the U.S. Senate for ratification, the U.S. Secretary of State suggested that these exceptions represent a "practical limit below which pollution has been shown in practical experiments to be negligible."[83] However, more recent investigations have demonstrated that many of the toxic aromatic hydrocarbons in oil are significantly water-soluble, are not broken down, and linger in the marine environment, then to be concentrated in the food chain. It is therefore probable to reason that the most significant damage to the marine environment is from the water-soluble parts of oil, and not from the visible element.[84] There may, in fact, be no "safe" levels of oil pollution.[85]

The 1969 amendments do not change the enforcement mechanism of the 1954 Convention. Signatory nations, although required under the 1954 Convention to impose penalties "adequate in severity to discourage" unlawful discharges, have been lax in their responsibility. Fines are light--U.S. implementing legislation imposes fines of not more than $2,500 for violations--and surveillance is scanty.

The Brussels Conventions

U.S. Senate Hearings on the 1969 Brussels conventions focused primarily on their relations to and effect upon the 1970 Water Quality Improvement Act. Outside the IMCO Conference, these hearings provide the most useful evaluations of the conventions.[86]

1969 Convention on Intervention on the High Seas in Cases of Oil Pollution Casualties

The absence of internationally agreed standards for pollution control promotes economic disadvantages for industries located in states with strong national pollution control legislation. It is not unusual to find industry joined with conservationists in states having such legislation to promote international acceptance of similar standards. Such was the case in the United States as experts representing normally conflicting interests testified in support of the Intervention Convention.

The Intervention Convention provides a desirable clarification of the questionable right of one nation to act against foreign vessels on the high sea. It allows nations to move more rapidly against oil pollution than they could "legally" have done in the past. Broad interpretation of the terms "grave and imminent danger" and "major harmful consequences" would, under the Intervention Convention, permit immediate and effective action in disasters like Torrey Canyon, in which a damaged oil tanker lies outside a nation's territorial jurisdiction but is polluting or threatens to pollute its shores and waters.

The conference that produced the convention recognized that "the limitation of the Convention to oil is not intended to abridge any right of a coastal state to protect itself against pollution by any other agent."[87] It further recommended that contracting states exercise their general law rights when confronted by pollution from any other agent. Essentially, the convention codified and extended to the high seas zone general customary international law requirements for the lawful exercise of the contemporary circumscribed right of self-help as applicable in the special case of averting the consequences of a catastrophic casualty at sea.[88]

The Convention on Civil Liability
for Oil Pollution Damage

The 1969 Brussels Private Law Convention represents the most recent of an emerging series calling for the imposition of strict liability for harms caused by extra-hazardous activities.[89] It signals an important step forward in the development of a "progressive" international law which seeks to acknowledge and address itself to the problem of "social costs." Enterprises engaged in high-risk programs--such as nuclear power development and the transportation of oil--may effectively expropriate public expectations of safety from harm when they neglect to assume the responsibilities for possible harm arising out of their activities. The value a society places on high-risk enterprises is expressed politically through a system of self-imposed limits on liability and claim against the enterprise.

Prior to the emergence of the Brussels Private Law Convention, 92 percent of the world's privately owned tanker fleet assumed risk through a private agreement known as the Tanker Owners Voluntary Agreement Concerning Liability for Oil Pollution (TOVALOP), which required participating tanker owners either to clean up oil spills caused by their negligence or to reimburse the government of a country whose shoreline was damaged or threatened by a spill. Under TOVALOP a tanker owner's liability was set at $100 per gross registered ton, but limited to $14 million per vessel per incident.[90] The similarity between the amount of liability under TOVALOP and the Private Law Convention indicated why the convention is so popular with most tanker owners, who exercise the most important influence behind intergovernmental negotiating positions, especially in IMCO. It is reasonable to conclude that the convention's passage was facilitated by the prior agreement of the tanker owners, and it is not unreasonable to assume that future extensions of liability will be heavily influenced by the direction private industry takes on a voluntary basis. CRISTAL--the Contract Regarding an Interim Supplement to Tanker Liability for Oil Pollution--provides guidance for the future of the international fund agreement that the Brussels Conference recommended be developed.[91] CRISTAL now binds approximately 80 percent of the international petroleum industry to provide additional funds for the extension of liability limits for each incident up to $30 million. This figure is now before the appropriate IMCO subcommittee studying the matter.

Two criticisms emerge within the context of liability. The first argues that by establishing equal access to the fund by three categories of claimants--governments, third parties, and owner-operators, to the extent that such may have expended funds to clean up the spill--the convention may seriously impair the rights of governments and third parties to a fund that may be exhausted by owner-operator clean-up costs alone. Torrey Canyon illustrated the convention's inadequacy. Under a tonnage formula as recommended, liability for that spill would have been limited to only $8 million. The case was settled at $7.6 million but required a very substantial compromise by the British and French governments, whose claims originally totaled over $16 million.[92]

The second criticism holds that the exclusivity of control recognized by the convention as pertaining to the flag state may exacerbate the "flags of convenience" approach. While in response to the first criticism convention proponents claim some protection is better than none, they generally acknowledge that the second presents severe problems. The possible tragic consequences of the emphasis may be seen in the registry of the PanHonLib Group (Panama, Honduras, and Liberia). Liberia, the flag state for the world's largest tanker fleet, is clearly incapable of enforcing antipollution measures against her own ships on the high sea even if she were to believe it in her particular interest to do so. Convention proponents urge that this major weakness not impede convention acceptance, and that instruments of law and policy be developed to safeguard coasts against these dangers.

Finally, many critics argue that the convention will preempt strong national legislation.[93] In extending the convention's provisions over the high seas, its drafters neglected to exempt the liability laws of states and regions that provide more strict third party liability. In the United States, for example, the absolute and unlimited liability for oil spills in Maine and Florida, which was specifically preserved in the 1970 Water Quality Improvement Act of 1970 amendments,[94] was preempted by the Senate's ratification of the convention. While uniform international law and jurisdiction is desirable, it is unfortunate that the convention did not include provisions allowing for parallel national legislation equal to or stronger than its own antipollution measures.

Several nations viewed the Brussels Conference generally, and the Convention Relating to Intervention in
Cases of Oil Pollution Casualties in particular, as an
attempt by the major maritime powers to limit rather than
progressively extend the rights of coastal states to act
outside their national zones of jurisdiction for the purpose of controlling marine pollution. Canada was particularly disillusioned with the conference and the unrespon-
sive approach of the international community to her particular needs. One Canadian spokesman, Foreign Minister
Mitchell Sharpe, said, "The outcome of the Brussels Conference . . . was so little oriented towards environmental
preservation and so much oriented in the interests of ship
and cargo owning States."

Based on her frustrating experience with law of the
sea processes, with defeat of many of her proposals at
both the 1958 Geneva and 1969 Brussels Conferences, and
with the imminency of extended oil tanker traffic through
the Northwest Passage as exemplified by the journey of
the U.S.S. Manhattan, Canada acted unilaterally on June 5,
1970, to protect her delicate Arctic ecology by extending
her contiguous zone to 100 miles above 60 degrees north
latitude for antipollution purposes by approving passage
of an Arctic Waters Pollution Prevention Act.[95]

Canada claimed that certain definitions of Article I
of the 1954 International Convention did not adequately
protect her interests. Her efforts to expunge the word
"heavy" from the diesel oil definition and to clarify the
definitions of oil to include certain oil-sand sludges
continually met with failure. Oil rigs were not included
in the convention, and the definitions of "grave and imminent" and "related interest" were not sufficient; the degree to which intervention might be taken was also uncertain, governed only by the vague rule of reasonableness,
and Canada's efforts to expand the degree also failed.

The Canadians contend that "all human activity in
the Arctic is potentially lethal" and that "in human
terms, the Arctic is a hemophiliac."[96] Wounds heal slowly, and ecologic illness is often progressive once in-
duced. The weight of scientific opinion indicates that
Arctic microscopic sea life is insufficient to cleanse
water exposed to a major oil spill, and that a spill from
a 200,000 or 300,000 ton oil tanker in Arctic waters would
persist for at least a century and possibly for a millen-
nium.[97] A multitude of irreplaceable faunal and floral
species would be eliminated. The most pessimistic view,

which has yet to be refuted, is that a blackening of thousands of square miles of the Arctic's surface could even result in a change of climatic patterns in southern regions of the Northern Hemisphere, with incalculable results to patterns of urban life in the populated regions of the globe.[98]

The Canadian Arctic Waters Pollution Prevention Act represents the most ambitious and extensive piece of unilateral antipollution law for the marine zone. By extending its contiguous zone to 100 miles from the coast north of the 60th parallel, Canada claimed it had made a positive contribution to customary international law. It cited the Truman Proclamation and other similar "protection" actions as ample precedent. The Canadian legislation was deliberately framed in terms of what had historically been deemed acceptable zone limitations for pollution control rather than in terms of contestable territorial sea claims.[99] Its authors referred to the 1954 Convention on Oil Pollution, as amended, and its authorized contiguous oil pollution zones of 100 nautical miles as the source of their determinations.[100]

Two basic attacks emerged against unilateral Canadian regulation of pollution in the Arctic waters. The first, contained in the U.S. government's formal protest, held that coastal jurisdiction does not exist for the high seas under any circumstances.[101] The second argued that the means of regulation were inconsistent with international standards for dealing with passage of ships, offshore drilling, or deep sea dredging.[102]

In combatting these arguments, Canada proposed that the right of innocent passage through straits--previously confirmed by the International Court of Justice (ICJ) in the Corfu Channel Case--is not applicable to its northern waters for two reasons: (1) the lack of customary passage and (2) the frozen geologic continuity and condition of the northern archipelagic islands. A number of comments by Canadian spokesmen may be read as going as far as suggesting that tanker passage, by virtue of its potential for pollution, may per se, be "non-innocent," in which case the question of whether the archipelagic waters are internal becomes moot.[103] Canadian spokesmen also pointed to the anomalous position of certain countries that, while prepared to admit that it is "permissible to sink a ship on the high seas after a marine accident has occurred which threatens pollution," continue to maintain that "it is not permissible to preclude that ship from entering certain areas in order to prevent an accident which would cause pollution."[104]

In taking the action, the Canadian government simultaneously registered a reservation at the United Nations
excluding Canada's acceptance of compulsory arbitration
and jurisdiction of the ICJ. Prime Minister Trudeau
stated:

> Canada is not prepared . . . to engage in
> litigation with other states . . . where
> the law is either inadequate or non-existent
> and thus does not provide a firm basis for
> judicial decision. . . . There is urgent
> need for the development of international
> law establishing that coastal states are
> entitled, on the basis of the fundamental
> principle of self defense, to protect their
> marine environment and the living resources
> of the sea adjacent to their coast.[105]

Supporters of the act argued that it was "justified
by the element of urgency in the need for protective
standards and procedures and by lingering deficiencies of
decision making in the international community." Critics
cited a "wave of nationalism, and not just the need to
protect the Arctic environment from pollution" as the
cause of the Canadian claim. Regardless of the legality
question, the Canadian action dramatized the inadequacy
of existing pollution law and spurred the United States
into convening an international conference on Arctic pollution problems. It also demonstrated the limited legal
recourse now available to states under international law
for self-protection from pollution.

Any survey of ICJ proceedings substantiates the near
legal void of precedent governing this area. States have
only three recourses. First, they may extend jurisdiction
to a twelve-mile contiguous zone as provided in the 1958
Geneva Conventions provided that international straits remain open to "innocent" passage. Such terms are open to
different interpretation and must be more clearly defined
in the future.

Second, states may request that a dispute be resolved
by an international tribunal. The most frequently cited
example of this method is the Trail Smelter Case, in which
an international tribunal held Canada responsible, as a
matter of customary international law, for pollution from
a smelting plant that was causing damage to property in
the United States. In the Trail case the court awarded
damages and ordered a cease-and-desist order until the
plant had installed adequate safeguards to prevent a

repetition of the damage. Such a method, however, is difficult to employ in a field where "damage" is not readily apparent and effects are incomplete. The burden of proof is on the plaintiff, who must prove serious consequences from a pollutant and who can expect no interim relief from pollution until after the case has been tried. Further international obligation seems to be limited to activities that threaten or injure the territory of another state. No enforceable obligation exists regarding damage to extremely valuable fishing or continental shelf interest located beyond territorial limits.[106]

Third, nation-states may seek relief from pollution damage in the courts of other states having appropriate jurisdiction. However, such actions are dependent on comity and rather narrowly limited under the concept of sovereign immunity when against the foreign state itself. Although many reciprocal arrangements allow foreign nationals to sue in other states, damages are limited for injury in some, and no injunctive relief is available in others.

International law writers have carefully documented a growing tendency of international law to accept the unilateral act of an interested nation in response to problems developed by new technologies, if not unreasonable, as presumptively lawful. This analysis and other surveys indicate that there is only one direction for emerging norms in the area of marine pollution control, namely toward effective regulation, and that in the absence of international controls, certain coastal states may prefer unilateral control measures to inaction.[107]

The International Law Commission and the Oil Pollution Convention itself both imply certain unilateral responsibilities: the former proposed a marine pollution liability concept specifically based on an express duty of individual interested states to take action in the absence of international agreement; the latter arguably authorized unilateral options on whether to pass both prescriptive and enforcement rules within 50 or 100 nautical miles from a nation's coast.[108]

The future course of international law development will, to a significant degree, depend on available institutions, interest group articulation, and the compromise of perceived national interests. Understanding existing international law and its development is important, but this alone is not a sufficient basis on which to develop model approaches to marine pollution control. Other possible determinant factors are discussed in the following chapters prior to final synthesis.

NOTES

1. D. W. Bowett, Law of the Sea (Dobbs Ferry, N.Y.: Oceana, 1967), p. 44. See also Myres S. McDougal and William T. Burke, The Public Order of the Oceans (New Haven: Yale University Press, 1962), pp. 1080-83 for severity regarding "stateless vessels."

2. Hugo Grotius, Mare Liberum, edited by James B. Scott (New York: Oxford University Press, 1916), p. 30.

3. Elizabeth Mann Borgese, The Ocean Regime (Santa Barbara, Calif.: Center for the Study of Democratic Institutions, October 1969), p. 24.

4. See Alison Reppy, "The Grotian Doctrine of the Freedom of the Seas Reappraised," Fordham Law Review 19 (1950).

5. William T. Burke, Toward a Better Use of the Ocean (New York: Humanities Press, 1969), p. 21.

6. Wolfgang Friedmann, The Future of the Oceans (New York: George Braziller, 1971), p. 6.

7. Burke, op. cit., pp. 6-7.

8. Ibid., p. 314.

9. Ibid., p. 36.

10. For an in-depth account of commission discussions, see McDougal and Burke, op. cit. For specific discussions, refer to various volumes of the Yearbook of the International Law Commission, UN Doc. No.a/CN.4 Ser. A./1950-56.

11. McDougal and Burke, op. cit., p. 670.

12. Ibid., p. 671.

13. J. P. François, Second Report on the High Seas, UN Doc. No. A/CN.4/42 (1951), p. 69.

14. Richard Young, "The Geneva Convention on the Continental Shelf: A First Impression," American Journal of International Law 52 (1958): 733, 735.

15. See commentary of Sir Gerald Fitzmaurice and Dr. Garcia-Amador in ILC Yearbook I (1956) (New York: United Nations Publication, 1956), pp. 134-35.

16. McDougal and Burke, op. cit., p. 687.

17. Ibid.

18. See Part II of the 1958 Geneva Convention on the Territorial Sea and Contiguous Zone. United Nations Conference on the Law of the Sea, Geneva, 1958. (London: Society of Comparative Legislation, 1958).

19. See Olivier de Ferron in Le Droit International de la Mer (Geneve: Droz, 1958), pp. 63-68.

20. O. D. Dickenson, "Jurisdiction at the Maritime Frontier," Harvard Law Review 40 (1920): 1, 15.

21. McDougal and Burke, op. cit., p. 620.

22. Sir Gerald M. Fitzmaurice, "The Law and Procedure of the International Court of Justice, 1951-54: Points of Substantive Law--I," British Yearbook of International Law 31 (1954): 371-79; Dean, "The Geneva Conference on the Law of the Sea: What Was Accomplished," American Journal of International Law 52 (1958): 607, 624.

23. See Bernard Margolis, "The Hydrogen Bomb Experiments and International Law," Yale Law Journal (1955): 629; McDougal, "The Hydrogen Bomb Tests and the International Law of the Sea," American Journal of International Law 49 (1955): 356.

24. 1956 ILC Yearbook, op. cit., p. 10, para. 52.

25. McDougal and Burke, op. cit., p. 759.

26. Ibid.

27. 1956 ILC Yearbook I, II, p. 33, para. 12, 15.

28. Ibid.

29. See 1958 Geneva conventions. (Note 18 supra.)

30. Soviet article stating, "States are bound to refrain from testing nuclear weapons on the high seas," UN Doc. No. A/ Conf. 13 C.2/ L. 30. (Unpublished mimeo.)

31. The object was to establish absolute prohibition and not incorporate the reasonableness criterion.

32. UN Doc. No. A/ Conf. 13 C 2/L.30, p. 143.

33. McDougal and Burke, op. cit., p. 855.

34. Lee Hydeman, ed., in Proceedings of the 1962 Conference on the Peaceful Uses of Atomic Energy (Vienna: IAEA, 1963), p. 305.

35. 1956 ILC Yearbook I, op. cit., p. 60, para 4.

36. Ibid., p. 31.

37. Ibid.

38. Ibid., Article 48 commentary, p. 31, para 4.

39. U.S. Government Interagency Coordinating Committee on Oceanography, "Study of Technical Aspects of ILC's Proposal Article 48: Pollution on the High Seas, 3" (Washington, D.C., mimeo., 1957), p. 6.

40. McDougal and Burke, op. cit., p. 865.

41. Official Records, 1958 Geneva Law of the Sea Conference, Vol. 4, p. 85. (Geneva, United Nations publication, 1968).

42. Ibid.

43. UN Doc. A/Conf.131/L.56.

44. U.S. Commission on Marine Science, Engineering and Resources, Panel Report, op. cit., Vol. II, pt. 2, Chap. 6, p. VIII-80.

45. Ibid., p. VIII-81.

46. McDougal and Burke, op. cit., p. 851.

47. Official Records, 1958 Geneva Law of the Sea Conference, op. cit., p. 138.

48. Bowett, *op. cit*., p. 45.

49. See IMCO, International Convention for the Pollution of the Sea by Oil, including amendments adopted in 1962 (London: IMCO, 1962), Annex A: Prohibited Zones, p. 22.

50. *Ibid*., Annex B.

51. *Ibid*., p. 8.

52. B. A. Boczek, *Flags of Convenience*: An International Legal Study (Cambridge, Mass.: Harvard University Press, 1962).

53. *Official Report* of the U.S. National Committee for the Prevention of Pollution of the Sea by Oil, Part II (Washington, D.C.: Department of State, 1968), p. 10.

54. IMCO Secretariat, "Activities of the IMCO in Relation to Marine Pollution," paper presented at the Fifth International Conference of the International Association on Water Pollution Research, San Francisco, July-August 1970.

55. See Convention, p. 6. (Note 18 *supra*.)

56. *Ibid*. Paraphrased from Article IV, p. 6.

57. Gerald Moore, "The Control of Marine Pollution and the Protection of Living Resources of the Sea: A Comparative Guide of International Controls and Rational Legislation and Administration" (Rome: FAO Technical Conference on Marine Pollution, 1970), FIR: MP/70/R-15, p. 2.

58. IMCO, "International Legal Conference on Marine Pollution Damage," final act of the Conference with attachments including the texts of the adopted conventions (London, 1969), p. 25.

59. *Ibid*.

60. *Ibid*., Article III (d), p. 26.

61. *Ibid*., Article III, p. 36, para. 1.

62. *Ibid*., Article V.

63. L. Leplat, "IMCO Combats Marine Pollution," *Marine Bulletin*, August 1970, p. 125.

64. See U.S. Commission on Marine Science, Engineering and Resources, *Panel Reports*, *op. cit*., pp. VII-84-90; Moore, *op. cit*.

65. *Ibid*., p. VIII-84.

66. Bowett, *op. cit*., p. 48.

67. *Ibid*., p. 47.

68. See United Kingdom/United States exchange of notes on June 19, 1964, *UK Treaty Series*, no. 37 (1964), Cmnd. 24111: The Limit of liability is $500 million, and the U.S. government agrees not to seek immunity from British courts.

69. Myres McDougal and Paul Schlei, "The H-Bomb Tests in Perspective: Lawful Measures for Security," Yale Law Journal 64 (1955): 686.

70. Bowett, op. cit., p. 49, reports that while the Japanese government condemned 176 tons of tuna, and tuna prices in Japan fell by 50 percent, no evidence exists that anyone was injured by consuming polluted fish. Miscalculation of the magnitude of the March 1, 1954, test explosion resulted in injury to 82 Marshallese on islands outside the warning zone and to the 27-man crew of the ill-fated Japanese fishing vessel Fukuryu Maru. The United States paid Japan $2 million damages, for both economic loss and injury to the fishermen, without ceding liability. Interference with shipping and air traffic was minimal.

71. U.S. Commission on Marine Science, Panel Report 3, op. cit., p. VIII-86.

72. Ibid.

73. U.S. Maritime Administration, Research and Development on Oil-Water Separator Systems (Washington, D.C.: Permutit, 1963).

74. James J. Reynolds, letter to Senator C. Pell dated May 28, 1971, in Brussels Convention Hearings, op. cit., p. 32.

75. Boczek, op. cit.

76. Official Report of the U.S. Committee for the Prevention of Pollution of the Sea by Oil (Washington, D.C.: Department of State, 1968), p. 5.

77. Ibid.

78. Ibid., p. 3.

79. Chief of Naval Operations, OPNAV INSTRUC 3/20. 21 A (Washington, D.C., August 3, 1968).

80. Eugene V. Coan, "Statement" at Hearings before the Foreign Relations Subcommittee on Oceans and International Environment of the U.S. Senate, 92nd Congress, 1st Session (May 20, 1971), p. 96.

81. Senator E. F. Hollings, "Statement" at Hearings before the Foreign Relations Subcommittee on Oceans and International Environment, op. cit., pp. 2-4.

82. Ibid.

83. Ibid., p. 101.

84. Blumer, op. cit.

85. Coan, op. cit.

86. Hearings before the Foreign Relations Subcommittee on Oceans and International Environment, op. cit.

87. Ibid., "Statement" of L. F. E. Goldie, p. 114.

88. _Ibid._, pp. 114-15. On the limited qualities of the right see Corfu Channel Case Judgment (1949) ICJ 4, 35; Brierly 425-26 in Shabtai Rosenne, _The Law and Practice of International Court of Justice_ (Leyden: A. W. Sijthoff, 1957), p. 138.

89. See L. F. E. Goldie, "Liability for Damage and the Progressive Development of International Law," _International and Comparative Law Quarterly_ 14 (1965): 11889, at 1226-31.

90. See Hearings before the Foreign Relations Subcommittee on Oceans and International Environment, _op. cit._.

91. See "Evaluation of the Proposed Civil Liability Convention of the IMCO by the Subcommittee on Air and Water Pollution of the House Committee on Public Works," Hearings before the Foreign Relations Subcommittee on Oceans and International Environment, _op. cit._, pp. 7-8.

92. _Ibid._, p. 96.

93. See, for example, Statement of Senator Edmund Muskie and exchange of letters with Deputy Attorney General Richard Kliendienst in Hearings before the Foreign Relations Subcommittee on Oceans and International Environment, _op. cit._.

94. For Maine statute, see "Oil Discharge Prevention and Pollution Control," Chapter 572, H.P. 1459-L.D. 1835, p. 79, Maine Legislative Service, Suppl. Maine Revised Statutes Annotated Public Laws, January-February 1970.

95. See Richard Bilder and Daniel Wilkes, works on Canadian Arctic Waters Pollution Prevention Act.

96. Paul St. Pierre, "Draft Report on the Threat of Ecologic Disaster in Arctic Regions" (Ottawa, Canada: North Atlantic Assembly, October 1970), p. 5.

97. _Ibid._, p. 9.

98. _Ibid_.

99. Daniel Wilkes, "International Administrative Due Process and Control of Pollution--The Canadian Arctic Waters Example," _Journal of Maritime Law and Commerce_, April 1971, p. 508.

100. See N. J. Healy and G. W. Paulsen, "Marine Oil Pollution and the Water Quality Improvement Act of 1970," _Journal of Maritime Law and Commerce_ 1 (1970): 537, 542ff.

101. For scholarly discussion of this issue, see L. M. Alexander, ed., _The United Nations and Ocean Management_ (Kingston: University of Rhode Island, Law of the Sea Institute, 1971) under titles Bilder, Johnston, LeGault, and Ratiner.

102. Wilkes, op. cit., p. 502.

103. Bilder, op. cit., p. 14.

104. Ibid.

105. St. Pierre, op. cit., p. 10.

106. Hydeman and Berman, in Proceedings of the 1964 Conference on the Peaceful Uses of Atomic Energy (Vienna: IAEA, 1965), p. 567.

107. Wilkes, op. cit., p. 505.

108. Preamble to Proposed Convention on Liability for Accidents contained in the report of J. Andrassy as "Etude des Mesures Internationales les Plus Aptes à Prévenir la Pollution des Milieux Maritimes," Institut de Droit International 12 (1969).

The debate on ocean resources, and hence on the
control of marine pollution, moved into what has been
termed the "articulation" stage when the UN General Assembly decided to convene a conference on the law of the sea
in 1973.[1] According to Assembly Resolution 2750 C (XXV),
one of the last items decided at the fall 1970 session,
the conference will consider:

> International machinery, for the area, and
> resources of the seabed and the ocean
> floor and the subsoil thereof beyond lim-
> its of national jurisdiction, a precise
> definition of the area, and a broad range
> of relative issues including those con-
> cerning the regimes of the high seas, the
> continental shelf, and territorial sea
> (including the question of international
> straits) and contiguous zone, fishing,
> and conservation of the living resources
> of the high sea (including the question of
> preferential rights of coastal states),
> the preservation of the marine environment,
> (including inter alia, the prevention of
> pollution and scientific research).[2]

The resolution reopened most, if not all, the topics
in the four 1958 Geneva conventions and required each government to develop positions on a number of issues.

Forces determining ocean policy can be ordered in a
variety of ways: As contending power groups in which

various interests seek to influence governments;[3] as political models, analogs, or constructs that provide the intellectual substructure for more specific schemes of allocating ocean resources;[4] or as the vital national interests of nation-states that cannot be compromised.[5] The interaction of these forces with the scientific nature of legal processes governing and institutional structures available for the control of marine pollution will determine its ultimate solution. While it is not necessary to comprehensively analyze these forces, they must be generally understood to realistically qualify and analyze the proposals they present within the context of marine pollution control. This chapter presents a view of the issues and forces in descending order of priority as presently viewed by the international community. How they are resolved will significantly affect the way marine pollution is controlled.

MILITARY AND STRATEGIC INTERESTS

National security and its attendant problems of military and strategic interests have been the most important issues for many nations in sea law conferences. For the more technologically advanced states, military security can be expected to be the first in any ranking of priorities.[6] Less developed countries that do not command large naval fleets have been interested in the extent to which security arrangements protect their exclusive controls, whether in the form of 200-mile territorial coastal zones, exclusive exploitation rights to continental margins, or exclusive environmental controls. No international regime for or conference about controlling marine pollution will be concluded without a satisfactory solution to the question of military and strategic uses of the seabed and the ocean space above.

There are two divergent concepts of the military use of the seabed.[7] The first gives the oceanbed the same legal status as the superjacent waters, and applies the same freedom to the seabed and the subsoil as to navigation on the high seas. Because warships of all nations have historically enjoyed the right to navigate on the high seas, it follows from such a conception that countries are equally free to use the oceanbed for naval purposes. The right to unilateral nuclear weapons testing or to dispose of obsolete munitions in the sea has not been resolved by international law.

The second concept reasons that since no usage or customs for the oceanbed have been developed, it must be considered a legal vacuum like outer space, for which laws must be developed by practice and international treaties. Use of the seabed for military or any other purpose beyond the limits of national jurisdiction is considered illegitimate under such a conception. Attempts were made in the UN General Assembly to limit such uses in November 1972. One proposal, advanced by Swedish delegate Alva Myrdal, was designed to encourage negotiations for an international regime that would be unencumbered by prior territorial claims or military occupations of portions of the seabed. Pending the outcome of negotiation, the proposal called upon states to refrain from "taking any measures with a view to appropriating any part of the ocean floor for military purposes."[8]

The moratorium resolution of the twenty-fourth UN General Assembly embodied this view. Resolution 254 D stated that states and persons "are bound to refrain from all activities of exploitation of the resources of the area of the seabed beyond the limits of national jurisdiction"[9] pending the establishment of an international regime. But some states expressed their unwillingness to be bound by the moratorium.

Although the prolonged discussions of the 18-nation UN Disarmament Committee have not produced any limitations on the use of the sea for submarines, they did conclude agreement on a joint minimum proposal to prohibit the installation of nuclear and other mass destruction weapons on the oceanbed. The prohibition was approved in treaty form by all but one (Mexico) of the 25 members of the Geneva Disarmament Talks on September 3, 1970. On November 17, 1970, the Political Committee of the United Nations approved the draft treaty by a vote of 91 to 2. Government spokesmen termed the treaty a significant step in the disarmament of the oceans. However, others noted that as long as mobile underwater warfare and weapons are allowed, the prohibition on fixed oceanbed installations will do little to diminish the danger of nuclear war and destruction from the sea.[10] While the proscription, if effective, will eliminate a possible source of radioactive contamination from the ocean environment, it was noted that remote stationing of such weapons might have been preferable to placing them close to concentrations of population.[11] In the end, however, informed judgment of cost and benefits rejected seabed emplacement beyond national jurisdiction.

The primary concern of the major powers is the maintenance of a credible nuclear deterrent. For the United States, the Soviet Union, and the United Kingdom, this deterrent has come to mean nuclear submarine fleets roving the high seas at will and undetected. Their military strategists emphasize the need for maximum maneuverability outside minimum territorial seas and for unhindered passage through international straits. A spokesman for the U.S. Department of Defense (DOD) stated:

> The new low profile posture requires more than ever that there be force mobility [and that] we [DOD] favor the narrowest possible area in which coastal states exercise sovereign rights to explore and exploit the seabeds. . . . We would prefer to trust the international community as a collective, than coastal states acting individually.[12]

Technological weapons developments continually decrease the proximate target distance required for these delivery systems. The MIRV (multiple independent reentry vehicles) and ULMS (underwater launching missile system) guided missile systems are capable of delivering payloads to targets over 6,000 miles from launch site. Thus, increased target distance capability and better sonar detection systems may render the unhindered passage through straits argument less important.[13]

Under the presently accepted three-mile limit of national jurisdiction, nuclear submarines can remain on station without surfacing for months. They remain undetected while submerged. Proposals to extend national jurisdiction to twelve miles or beyond significantly affect and circumscribe a submarine's freedom of maneuverability, as well as increasing the chances of detection. Without a provision for free passage through straits and narrows, submarines would be required under the 1958 Geneva Convention of the Territorial Sea to surface and fly their flags when passing through the territorial waters of another state. A 12-mile extension would affect 116 straits, including the Straits of Gibraltar.[14] A 200-mile extension would close off the Mediterranean, the Baltic, the Sea of Japan, the South China Sea, and all passages to the Arctic, the Caribbean, and the Gulf of Mexico; it would also cut the USSR from direct access to the Atlantic.[15]

The military interest in sea law and international regimes is not limited to the maximum maneuverability-minimum territorial sea arguments of conventional naval warfare. Nor do military strategists present a united approach before government policy-making groups. The interests of different branches of service, while not completely in conflict, often require difficult compromises in government positions. The classic dichotomy among military strategists can be observed in the American policy-making process. Particular circumstances may be different in other advanced countries, but the model is probably valid for all major naval powers.

Competing within the military establishment are two philosophically different, but not technically opposite, power groups. One is represented by the "flexible response-gunboat diplomacy" advocates, who argue the maximum maneuverability-minimum territorial principle for purposes other than strictly nuclear submarine warfare. They base their case on the obsolescence of conventional war and the tendency of nations today to use the least amount of force necessary to secure national goals rather than risk nuclear war by concentrating the maximum force available.[16] In limited war situations, they argue, emphasis must be placed on strategic mobility. To apply effective pressure, governments must be able to move forces into positions as quickly and efficiently as possible, and to place them in an obvious and visible striking position. In the absence of this kind of mobility, major powers would be required to maintain large and credible forces stationed in foreign lands. But it has been demonstrated that the maintenance of such forces is not only a drain on a nation's balance of trade but also a risky political problem for democratically elected allies. There is also evidence that it is often both easier and faster to move men from the United States to any part of the world than to move them shorter distances from advanced bases in foreign countries.[17]

Extending national jurisdictions to 12 or 200 miles would severely limit the mobility of warships through neutral territorial waters under the "innocent passage" provisions of the Geneva conventions. Lines of supply (if they could be developed) and mileage costs (if not prohibitive) would severely hamper any such operations. Without such lines the time on station, so critical to operations like the Cuban missile quarantine, would be cut short.[18] Finally, the psychological impact of "showing the flag" at a <u>visible</u> three-mile limit may be much greater than at a 12- or certainly a 200-mile limit.

The other side of the military argument is detection and intelligence. To keep track of missile-carrying submarines, major powers employ active and passive sonar listening devices, some of which are positioned on the deep ocean floor and on the bottoms of continental shelves.[19] Cables run from the devices to shore, providing links for power and monitoring. Intelligence personnel engaged in this kind of activity use the continental shelf convention as an argument to keep others from working near equipment mounted on the bottom beyond the territorial sea but within the jurisdiction of the shelf convention.[20] Those charged with the task of maintaining surveillance of enemy submarines would "prefer a new territorial sea convention or at least a continental shelf convention that extended seaward to a depth of at least 2,000 meters."[21]

It has been suggested that provisions be made for the priority and protection of military uses of the sea floor as part of a general regime for the ocean, provided the state concerned gives notice:

> on an analogy with the relevant Trustee-
> ship Articles of the United Nations Charter,
> states seeking to establish fixed defense
> installations on sea mounts and on the sea-
> bed should give notice to the effect that
> such areas are taken for defense purposes
> and are not to be viewed as being any
> longer within the general regime of the
> seabed and its subsoil. Upon such an an-
> nouncement the state in question may
> further establish security zones.[22]

While the reporting procedure would not be mandatory, military installations and activities otherwise emplaced or conducted would not have the benefits of the proposed regime, and in particular would be subordinated to resource exploitation carried out under the general regime proposed.[23] Any use intended to be covert that is uncovered in the course of mineral resource exploration or exploitation, or any other use of the seabed or its subsoil, would presumably lose its value.[24] In the event that overt military use of an area of the deep sea could not be accommodated with mineral resource exploration or exploitation under a claim registered or sought with an international registry authority, one national policy panel recommends:

> that if the overt military use was prior
> in time, it shall prevail, but the State

making such preclusive military use of the
area shall pay an appropriate amount to
[an] International Fund. If registered
mineral resources exploration or exploitation was prior in time, it shall prevail,
unless the State wishing to make the military use purchases the rights of the State
Registrant and pays an appropriate amount
to the International Fund.[25]

Security considerations were a major force in shap-
ing community policy that placed the continental shelf
under coastal jurisdiction for the purposes of resource
exploration and exploitation. The major maritime powers
will be unwilling to accept an international regime for
regulating ocean uses beyond the shelf unless some means
can be devised to accommodate military activities on the
sea floor with other uses of that region.[26] It has been
suggested that such uses should be regarded as reasonable,
subject to the requirement of relatively slight interference with navigation or any other inclusive use of the
shelf region.[27] Preoccupation with the more difficult
and perhaps unattainable goal of complete prohibition of
military use may well be the most important obstacle to
agreement on an international regulatory system for commercial development and, ipso facto, marine pollution.[28]

Conclusion

The requirements of national security and comprehensive marine pollution control are not mutually exclusive.
The major naval powers are more concerned over free transit through certain straits and narrow seas than with the
precise width of the territorial sea and the continental
shelf.[29] Amendments to the High Seas Convention designed
to control marine pollution must incorporate provision
for free transit through international straits if they
are to receive the support of the major naval powers. No
international law of the sea is effective unless it is enforceable.[30]

FISHERIES INTERESTS

Debate over future sea law has focused almost entirely on the breadth of territorial seas and its effect on

military interests, and on the seabed and its accessibility to mineral exploitation; the problems of international marine fisheries have been either ignored or explicitly rejected.[31] Although nation-states continue to deliberately avoid the fishing issue in context with other major uses of the sea, it is highly probable that the next law of the sea conference will be charged with the burden of attempting to establish, by one method or another, a limit on exclusive coastal control over fisheries.[32] This reluctance of the international community has been based largely on the fear that a conference would be unable to agree on a fishing limit and that failure in this area would jeopardize other important negotiations rather than on the priority and economic value of world fisheries. Fishery matters have become entangled with other issues more intimately connected with power considerations. But as the Icelandic cod war demonstrates, no issue is more volatile or immediately important to the international community than fishing rights. No satisfactory law of the sea can be established until this potential for conflict has been defused.

The growing importance of marine sea foods to the world community can be seen in Figure 3.1. Fishing increased from a few million tons at the beginning of the century to about 15 million tons in 1938. It doubled in twenty years, reaching 27 million tons in 1958, then doubled again in ten years, reaching 56 million tons in 1969. Considering the remarkable development of fishing technology--the use of sonar and satellites for fish location, new fishing gear, midwater trawlers, mechanized devices for net handling--it is likely that total fish production, from inland and marine waters for human and animal consumption, will reach 74 million tons by 1975 and 107 million tons by 1985 (excluding the development of "unconventional species such as the Antarctic krill, or the somewhat unpredictable potential of aquaculture and fish farming"[33]).

The potential sustainable yield of sea food is estimated at 200 million tons a year, which could provide the earth's population with about one-third of its total protein requirement by the year 2000.[34] Fish is the primary source of animal protein for nations with low nutritional levels, filling the gap between starvation and subsistence for more millions of people than either meat or milk. More than two-thirds of all meat and milk is consumed by less than 600 million people, but over 1.5 billion people depend on aquatic food for more than one-half of their average animal protein.[35]

FIGURE 3.1

Productivity of Marine Fisheries

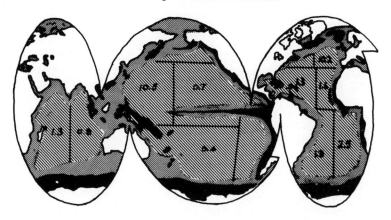

▨ Very high biological productivity ▨ Medium biological productivity
■ Low biological productivity

Productivity of marine fisheries. The number that appears within
each oceanic subdivision indicates the quantity (in metric tons) of fish
landed in 1967.

Area	Millions of tons	% of total catch	Area	Millions of tons	% of total catch
NW Atlantic	4.0	7.6	N Pacific	6.4	12.2
NE Atlantic	10.2	19.5	W Central Pacific	10.5	20.0
W Central Atlantic	1.3	2.5	E Central Pacific	0.7	1.3
E Central Atlantic	1.6	3.1	SE Pacific	11.2	21.5
SW Atlantic	1.3	2.5	SW Pacific	0.4	0.8
SE Atlantic	2.5	4.8	E Indian Ocean	0.8	1.5
			W Indian Ocean	1.3	2.5

Year	Landings
1950	21.1
1951	23.1
1952	25.1
1953	25.9
1954	27.6
1955	28.9
1956	30.4
1957	31.5
1958	33.2
1959	36.7
1960	40.0
1961	43.4
1962	46.9
1963	48.2
1964	52.5
1965	53.3
1966	56.8
1967	51.5 (estimate)

Total world catch, 1950-67 (millions of metric tons). Source:
Data from Food and Agriculture Organization of the United Nations,
Yearbook of Fishery Statistics, 1966 (1968).

95

Politically, fishing interests are expressed in a number of ways: in the proportionate value of the industry to a nation's economy; in its "relative" value to other major uses (military, mineral, transportation); and in its value relative to foreign diplomacy. The relative importance of fisheries to a nation can be determined by catch levels and consumption. Japan, for example, consumes 67 pounds per capita, the Scandinavian countries about 45 pounds. The United States consumes only 11 pounds per capita (ranking sixth in tons of fish caught, behind Peru, Japan, the USSR, the People's Republic of China, and Norway).[36] Other countries base their interests on new scientific theories concerning fish and other industries.[37] Peru, for example, advanced a "biological complex" or "bioma" theory, asserting that depletion of anchovy by overfishing leads to a breakdown in the anchovy-cormorant-guano relationship, depletion of bird flocks, and hence a decrease in the guano deposits that are so vital to the Peruvian economy.[38]

Fishing interests can be broken into three groups: the food fish processing industry, the fish meal industry, and the fish catching industry, which in turn can be divided into coastal and distant water fisheries. Each group has different short-term goals that they articulate through national policy-making mechanisms. Generally, coastal industries that fish in international waters contiguous to their coasts press their governments to extend national jurisdiction or sovereignty over their fishing zones to the maximum extent possible. Exclusive fishing zones and rights have been extended beyond the normally acceptable three-mile limit of national jurisdiction from 12 to 200 miles. On the other hand, distant water fisheries that operate in international waters contiguous to other coasts lobby within their national policy-making processes for minimum extensions of coastal state jurisdiction and maximum freedom of the sea. The processing and fish meal industries support whichever type of fishing industries provide their raw materials.

Highly developed nation-states tend to favor regional fishery arrangements that recognize previous use and abstention for the sake of conservation and that restrict entry into fishing grounds and give priority to nations that have constrained their own fishermen to preserve stocks.[39] Less developed nations seek to protect their potential wealth by declarations of sovereign jurisdiction over their coastal resources or by refusing to recognize "discriminatory" regulations that favor existing fisheries and restrict entry into certain grounds.

Most experts agree that in considering the future of fishery regulations around the world the most important task is to specify preferential goals. Without some conception of goals or objectives, assessment of the various alternatives is obviously very difficult. William Burke has suggested the following goals for the international community:

1. The preservation of minimum order and the avoidance of violent conflict.
2. Wider distribution of benefits of fishery exploitation.
3. Increased production of protein.
4. Maintenance of physical yield from the ocean.
5. Improving economic benefits from fisheries.[40]

The Geneva Convention on the Conservation of the Living Resources of the Sea and a collection of bilateral fishing commissions have been inadequate instruments of international fishery management; unless they are improved or new institutions and agreements are established, the short-term economics of a highly technological and competitive industry will prevail and the likelihood of attaining the "community" goals will be reduced. Without a satisfactory international agreement on a territorial sea limit for fishery purposes, many states have proceeded to unilaterally promulgate jurisdiction zones for fisheries purposes.[41] While these limits may vary, the pressure of existing claims may foreclose backtracking and de facto render a 200-mile limit the only largest common denominator.

The conservation of fisheries within these "special purpose zones" would eventually include the control of pollution. Overfishing is no longer the only activity requiring regulation. If the international community grants coastal states jurisdiction over fisheries, it will have to make clear whether or not that control explicitly or implicitly implies control of pollution.

TRANSPORTATION INTERESTS

The objectives of the transportation industry--whether container ships, tramp freighters, or jumbo tankers--are similar for the purposes of lobbying on law and the sea: to move goods as simply, quickly, cheaply, and safely as possible. To achieve these goals the industry can be expected to support any proposals that will furnish better charts and navigational aids, or will generally

enhance safe and efficient transportation. On the other
hand, it can also be expected to oppose international
regimes that impede or increase shipping costs, and to
block any erosion of the present rule on innocent passage
through straits.

A major problem could develop for the transportation
industry if other nations followed Canada's lead in unilaterally establishing regulations for pollution zones.
Nations that are heavily dependent on ocean transportation
have given this interest a high priority and have pressed
for internationally agreed standards. The transportation
industry shares the military's interest in preserving traditional freedoms of the sea.

"SOFT" MINERAL INTERESTS

National and international oil and gas industries
are the strongest organized private interest groups seek-
ing to shape government and international policy regarding the seabed. The petroleum industry played an important role in formulating the Truman Proclamation of 1945,
which claimed the nonliving resources of the continental
shelf for the United States and led to the 1958 Law of
the Sea Conference in Geneva.[42] The influence of the
Truman Proclamation is international in scope. Although
most petroleum resources are under dry land, there are
now in excess of 16,000 offshore wells in the United
States alone, with drilling under way in at least 28
other countries.[43] While the world value of fish landed
is more than twice the value of crude oil from offshore
drilling sites, the present growth rate indicates that in
fifteen years the world dollar value of offshore petroleum
will be considerably larger than the world dollar value of
fisheries (see Figure 3.2).

Oil and natural gas companies have three basic requirements to exploit offshore resources efficiently.
First, they must have security of tenure--security that
once they pay someone royalties and invest money into an
operation, they can continue their operations without in-
terferences or sudden stoppages. Second, they require a
guarantee that individual companies rather than individual
nations be allowed to apply for and obtain licenses under
some form of regulatory authority. Third, they would prefer that property allocations proceed with all reasonable
speed since the logistics and risk capital required in
such undertakings require reasonable timetables.

FIGURE 3.2

Value of Resources Extracted
from the Sea by United States, 1960-67

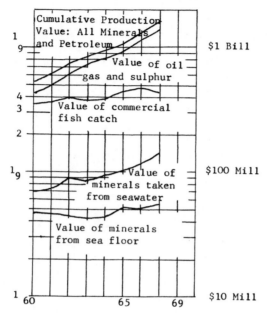

In most countries the oil industry speaks officially
with one voice and avoids the policy conflict of the fishing industry. The petroleum industry maintains a high degree of issue integrity for a number of reasons: There
are no divergent interests; foreign subsidiaries align
with the policy of the mother country; and stock ownership is spread out among the international community.

Official views of the international petroleum industry often parallel those of the U.S. National Petroleum
Council (NPC), whose position, affirmed in its 1969 report, has been that "national jurisdiction extends over
the continental rise."[44] In the NPC's view the best interests of oil companies are served under existing principles of international law by which nation-states may
promptly and rightly assert jurisdiction over the rise
and recognize the right of other coastal nations to do
the same. It was further agreed that such extensions of
national jurisdiction could be implied from the history
of the discussion leading to the continental shelf convention, and that a distinctly different geology differenti-
ates the deep ocean floor from the continental land masses.

TABLE 3.1

Potential U.S. and World Petroleum Resources

Area	Remaining Proved Reserves (billions of barrels or trillions of cubic feet)			Recoverable Resources (under current economics and technology, including cumulative production and proved reserves)		
	Crude Oil	Natural Gas	NGL	Crude Oil	Natural Gas	NGL
Total United States	31	286	8	547	2,737	82
Continental United States	27	255	7	367	1,838	55
U.S. continental shelves (total)*	4	31	1	180	900	27
Total world except United States	357	786	NA	1,575	13,250	355
Total world	388	1,073	NA	2,122	15,987	437

Note: Figures are calculated from data to January 1, 1966.

*Continental shelves include state land or 0 to 2,500 meters isobath.

Source: Data drawn from V. E. McKelvey et al., "Potential Mineral Resources of the United States Outer Continental Shelves" (unpublished report of the Geological Survey to the Public Land Law Review Commission, March 1968).

100

John Knauss believes there are three primary reasons
for the NPC position:
    1. There would appear to be large quantities of
petroleum in the continental margins. Although the deep
sea floor is not ruled out as a possible source of petroleum reserves, the amount per unit area will be less and
the technology for exploitation is some time off.
    2. Some form of stable legal regime is necessary be-
fore the industry could be expected to make the large in-
vestments necessary to develop these resources. Since the
present regime of national jurisdiction has led to successful development of offshore resources, it seems better
to go with a known system that has worked than with an unknown system that no one has yet described adequately.
    3. The United States has large continental margins,
and although its gain in potential resources may not be
proportionately as great as some other countries, the
United States will fare rather well under the NPC proposal. It has also been suggested that the large international petroleum corporations will gain a U.S. tax advantage under the NPC proposal.[45]
    The NPC position cannot be sustained as a simple ex-
tension of the exploitability criterion of the Geneva
Shelf Convention. Nor does its assertion of an accurate
geologic boundary necessarily apply to limits of national
jurisdiction. Boundaries have often been determined
more by pragmatic reasons than because of their geologic
implications. Those within the industry who argue against
the NPC position suggest that it may be in their best interest to establish an international regime, provided it
is free from the major weaknesses of international organizations. Moreover, major maritime states would find themselves without any substantial control over or access to
the floor of the sea under the NPC proposal, merely because deep-rooted accidents of history would give major
possession to states holding distant islands groups (see
Chapter 2, Figure 2.3).
    Energy shortages and projections of dependence on im-
ported oil have strengthened the industry's argument while
bringing it into conflict with the military, which generally favors minimum territorial limits. Resolving that
conflict continues to tax the ingenuity of those who wish
the resources of the sea floor to be under national jurisdiction and the water column above to be international.
And while the industry would prefer coastal control for
pollution control, it would advocate internationally
agreed standards.

"HARD" MINERAL INTERESTS

Most observers believe serious deep sea mining operations will take place within the decade.[46] The hard metal
industry has focused its interest on both the shallow and
deep ocean. Placer deposits of tin, diamonds, gold, and
platinum can be found in submerged stream channels in
depths of less than 200 meters, but the possible extraction of copper, nickel, and cobalt found in manganese
nodule concentrations on the ocean floor attracts the
most interest due to its economic feasibility.

In contrast to the petroleum industry's "do-nothing"
approach, certain mining interests have urged their governments to proceed with international arrangements beyond the limits of national jurisdiction. The most powerful of these, the American Mining Congress, has called
for a precise definition of the boundary between national
and international jurisdiction, for the formulation of improved national rules on area jurisdiction, and for the
earliest possible formulation of precise international arrangements and legal principles regarding the development
of deep ocean mining.[47] But at present the industry lacks
complete knowledge of ocean environments and the technology required to economically exploit these resources. As
a result, the industry has not been able to formulate specific recommendations on means of allocating seabed resources so as to facilitate both the orderly, peaceful development of such resources and their productive, rational
exploitation. Some frequently mentioned alternatives are:
1. Division of the oceanbed among coastal states.
2. Provision for completely free access, leaving
assurance of rights, the adjustment of conflicts, and the
accommodation with other uses to be resolved as contro-
versy arises and in accordance with other available international law principles.
3. Establishment of an international agency, based
on one already in existence or to be created, to allocate
rights among claimants and to regulate exploitation.
4. Provision for an international recording system,
leaving regulation to national systems of law.
5. Provision for exploration and exploitation to be
undertaken by public international groups on behalf of
all states.[48]
Of these five policy alternatives, most officials
tend to disregard 1 and 5: the first because major maritime states would find themselves without any substantial
control over access to the floor of the sea because of

deep-rooted accidents of history that give major possession to states holding distant island groups; the fifth
because of the crucial elements of capital availability
and skill now in the hands of private groups, which some
states are unlikely to divert into an international agency.
Mining groups are likely to finalize their bargaining position somewhere between these two extremes according to
what best protects and rewards investment.

NOTES

1. Michael Haas, "A Functional Approach to International Organization," The Journal of Politics 27 (1965):
502.
2. UN Resolution 2750 (XXV), adopted December 17,
1970.
3. See John A. Knauss, "Factors Influencing a U.S.
Position in a Future Law of the Sea Conference" (Kingston:
Law of the Sea Institute, University of Rhode Island, Occasional Paper No. 10, April 1971).
4. See Robert L. Friedheim, "Understanding the Debate on Ocean Resources" (Denver: University of Denver,
Graduate School of International Affairs, World Affairs
Monograph Series, 1969).
5. See Margaret Lynch Gerstyle, "The Politics of
U.N. Voting" (Kingston: Law of the Sea Institute, University of Rhode Island, Occasional Paper No. 7, July
1970).
6. Knauss, op. cit., p. 2.
7. Wolfgang Friedham, The Future of the Oceans (New
York: George Braziller, 1971), pp. 50-61.
8. Gerstyle, op. cit., p. 4.
9. W. Friedham, op. cit., p. 53.
10. Bruce A. Harlow, "Freedom of Navigation," in
L. M. Alexander, ed., The Law of the Sea (Columbus: Ohio
State Press, 1967).
11. Ibid.
12. Robert A. Frosch, Hearings on Senate Joint Res.
111, Senate Resolutions 172 and 186, statement before Senate Committee on Foreign Relations, 90th Congress, 1st
Session (1967), p. 39.
13. Knauss, op. cit., p. 4.
14. D. K. Paht, War in the Deterrent Age (A. S.
Barnes, 1966).
15. See J. I. Caffey, Technology and Strategy in
Mobility in the Implications of Military Technology in

the 1970's, Adelphi Papers, No. 46 (London: The Institute of Strategic Studies, 1968).

16. See Herbert York, "Military Technology and National Security," Scientific American, August 1969.

17. See P. Vigoureaux and J. B. Hersey, "Sound in the Sea," in M. N. Hill, ed., The Sea, Vol. I (Interscience, 1962).

18. Knauss, op. cit., p. 5.

19. Ibid.

20. L. F. E. Goldie, in Alexander, ed., op. cit.

21. Ibid., p. 284.

22. U.S. Commission of Marine Science, Engineering and Resources, Panel Reports, Vol. 3: Marine Resources and Legal Political Arrangements for Their Development (Washington, D.C.: U.S. Government Printing Office, 1969).

23. Ibid., p. VIII-43.

24. William T. Burke, Towards a Better Use of the Oceans (Stockholm: Almquist and Wiksell, 1969), pp. 91-99.

25. Myres S. McDougal and William T. Burke, The Public Order of the Oceans (New Haven: Yale University Press, 1962), p. 724.

26. W. T. Burke, op. cit., p. 113.

27. Knauss, op. cit., p. 8.

28. See Bernard Oxman, "Report on the President's Proposal," in Alexander, ed., op. cit., p. 167.

29. See Alexander, ed., op. cit., for discussion.

30. Ibid.

31. Francis T. Christy, "Fisheries and the New Convention of the Law of the Sea," in Alexander, ed., op. cit., p. 455.

32. W. T. Burke, "Some Thoughts on Fisheries and a New Conference on the Law of the Sea" (Kingston: Law of the Sea Institute, University of Rhode Island, Occasional Paper No. 9, March 1971).

33. Elizabeth Mann Borgese, "The Seas: A Common Heritage," in The Center Magazine (Center for the Study of Democratic Institutions) 4, no. 2 (March/April 1972): 18.

34. Ibid.

35. Ibid.

36. Knauss, op. cit., p. 8.

37. Ibid.

38. Thomas Wolff, "Peruvian-U.S. Relations Over Maritime Fishing: 1945-1969" (Kingston: Law of the Sea Institute, University of Rhode Island, Occational Paper No. 4, March 1970), p. 6.

39. *Marine Resources and Legal Political Arrange-ments for Their Development*, *op. cit.*, pp. VIII-50-51.

40. W. T. Burke, *op. cit*.

41. *Ibid*., p. 14.

42. See progressive position papers of National Petroleum Council.

43. *Marine Resources and Legal Political Arrange-ments for Their Development*, *op. cit*.

44. National Petroleum Council, *Report* on offshore resources (1969).

45. Senator Claiborne Pell, *Hearings* Before House Subcommittee on Oceanography, August 5, 1969.

46. Knauss, *op. cit*., p. 15.

47. "Declaration of Policy 1970-7-," adopted by American Mining Congress, September 27, 1970.

48. See Lewis Alexander, ed., *Proceedings* Law of the Sea Institute, 1969 (Kingston, Rhode Island: University of Rhode Island, 1969).

CHAPTER

4

THE ORGANIZATIONS

There are a large number of international organizations involved with the problems of marine pollution. Within the United Nations system, in addition to the United Nations itself, are several organizations dealing with the varied but interrelated aspects of marine pollution: UNESCO (the UN Educational, Scientific and Cultural Organization), and its Inter-Governmental Oceanographic Commission (IOC), the Food and Agricultural Organization (FAO), World Health Organization (WHO), World Meteorological Organization (WMO), Inter-Governmental Maritime Consultative Organization (IMCO), and International Atomic Energy Agency (IAE). Their activities in the whole area of marine affairs, including pollution, have been carried out mainly along sectoral lines. Each organization has considered the problem from its own point of view and, quite naturally, has proposed programs designed to enhance its reputation and increase its budget.

No specialized agency or intergovernmental organization has claimed terms of reference wide enough to provide overall competence and guidance on the subject. All receive scientific advice from the Joint Group of Experts on the Scientific Aspects of Marine Pollution (GESAMP), which they jointly established and support. Several organizations cooperate with IOC in the implementation of the Long-Term and Expanded Program of Oceanic Exploration and Research (LEPOR). All provided advice and assistance to the preparatory committee of the 1972 United Nations Human Environment Conference and to the United Nations Committee on the Peaceful Uses of the Sea-Bed in its preparations for the 1973-74 Law of the Sea Conference.

Outside the United Nations system, a number of standing governmental and nongovernmental organizations have evidenced concern and activity in the area of marine pollution control. These include the North Atlantic Treaty Organization (NATO) Committee on the Challenges of Modern Society, the Organization for Economic Cooperation and Development (OECD), and the International Council for Scientific Unions (ICSU). Other groups such as the International Council for the Exploration of the Sea, the International Union for Conservation of Nature and Natural Resources, the European Economic Community (EEC), and the UN Economic Commission for Europe have engaged to a lesser extent in activities related to the international control of marine pollutants.

This chapter summarizes the activities and programs of these international organizations as they pertain to ocean pollution. The purpose of the summary is to indicate the degree of fragmentation in jurisdiction, competence, and ability to cope with marine pollution on the international organizational level, and to suggest changes that would provide a clear and unified approach to the problem. The primary emphasis is to indicate the need for change; the practical problems of how should best be reserved for reorganization experts.

UNESCO AND ITS INTER-GOVERNMENTAL OCEANOGRAPHIC COMMISSION

The activities of UNESCO and its Inter-Governmental Oceanographic Commission (IOC) are primarily concerned with the scientific investigation of physical, chemical, and biological processes in the ocean. Its role in the international control of marine pollution therefore focuses on the routes, fates, and effects of pollutants, and the problems of monitoring them. UNESCO's activities have been divided into three main categories: individual assistance to member states; the promotion of collective advancements in methodology, training, research, and information services; and assistance for concerted action through support of the IOC.[1] The United Nations has encouraged developing countries to conduct baseline ecological monitoring of the marine environment and to conduct investigations of manmade changes through Development Program Technical Assistance projects. UNESCO efforts to promote marine pollution investigation methodology have included joint sponsorship of a seminar on methods of detection, measurement, and monitoring; assistance to expert working groups of the Special Committee on Oceanic Research; and contracts with the IAEA laboratory of marine radioactivity in Monaco.

Until 1955 the only marine science work in the United Nations system took place in the FAO, but in the judgment of some scientists it was not then sufficiently oriented toward the physical science aspects of oceanography. The science sector of UNESCO seemed to offer a more congenial home for oceanographers and the added attraction of USSR membership, which FAO lacks.[2] International oceanographic activity began to gravitate toward UNESCO as official governmental representatives debated the pros and cons of how international marine science should be organized. That debate ended in 1960, when the UN General Assembly passed Resolutions 2414 and 2467 establishing the programs of LEPOR (Long-Term and Expanded Program of Ocean Exploration and Research) and IDOE (International Decade of Oceanic Exploration) under IOC auspices.

IOC was early recognized as the international forum for sea pollution investigations. One of the earliest comprehensive reports on pollution of the sea was submitted to IOC at its fourth session in Paris in November 1965, by the Centre Scientifique de Monaco.[3] Pursuant to the report's recommendations, IOC established a working group on marine pollution which met for the first time in August 1967 in Paris. The group concluded "that the time has come to treat all kinds of marine pollution . . . as facets of a single problem requiring concerted action by chemists, radio-chemists, marine biologists, and microbiologists, physical and chemical oceanographers, engineers, lawyers, administration, etc."[4]

To efficiently study and eliminate pollution, the working group recommended that the fifth IOC sessions:

1. Draw the attention of the IOC members to the need for further research and dissemination of information on oceanographic and other related aspects of marine pollution.

2. Request IOC members to arrange to have research conducted on a continuing basis, to share their experience and information on problems of marine pollution with one another, and to maintain records of discharges.

3. Request the interested organizations of the UN family to agree on appropriate machinery to ensure joint action in the field of marine pollution, including a system for regular reporting by national sources to appropriate regional or international bodies of discharges of

pollutants and the maintenance of an international registry of same.[5]

The working group also prepared a table of major categories of pollution and a description of the various pollutants and their sources.[6]

IOC's fifth session noted these recommendations and adopted Resolution V-19, agreeing to reconsider the position of its working group on marine pollution if an alternative scientific group under the joint sponsorship of interested United Nations organizations were established. When a Joint IMCO/FAO/UNESCO/WMO Group of Experts on the Scientific Aspects of Marine Pollution (GESAMP) was established, IOC dissolved its working group and arranged to delegate representatives to future meetings of GESAMP.[7]

IOC activity on marine pollution did not end with the formation of GESAMP. In response to UN General Assembly Resolution 2467 (XXIII) of December 1968 requesting UNESCO and IOC to intensify their activities in the scientific field of coordinating a long-term and expanded program of worldwide exploration of the oceans and their resources, a special working group was established by the IOC Bureau and Consultative Council in June 1969 to prepare a draft comprehensive outline of the program's scope.[8] The purpose of the expanded program was recognized as follows: "to increase knowledge of the ocean . . . and to improve understanding of processes operating in or affecting the marine environment, with the goal of enhanced utilization of the ocean and its resources for the benefit of mankind."[9] The draft included marine pollution in the scientific content of the expanded program.[10] It stated that all sources of pollutants should be monitored, understood, and controlled as far as possible, and that scientific studies in the following areas could lead to the preparation of periodic comprehensive reports on the ocean's health:

1. Study of the changes in the marine environment and the impact on marine life from pollution.

2. Investigation of the delayed and sublethal effects of pollutants that are not always immediately apparent.

3. Development of standardized methods of analysis for pollutants and identification of a spectrum of species that are sensitive indicators of pollutant levels in different areas.

4. Establishment of a worldwide system of monitoring and sample collection.

5. Provision of the scientific basis for methods of removing or countering the deleterious effects of pollutants in the sea.[11]

To further the development of LEPOR, IOC established a Group of Experts on Long-Term Scientific Policy and Planning (GELTSPAP) which, at its first session, proposed that a Global Investigation of Pollution in the Marine Environment (GIPME) be included in LEPOR as a matter of high priority. IOC's Bureau and Consultative Council adopted the GELTSPAP recommendations and passed them along to IOC's seventh session, which met in late 1971. The specific proposals on the organization and work program of GIPME were taken up at this meeting. They indicated that such an investigation would require the establishment of baseline stations in representative areas of the oceans to assess the state and trends of chemical contamination.

The Integrated Global Ocean Station System (IGOSS), sponsored by IOC in cooperation with WMO, has also been proposed as part of the design of pollution monitoring systems. IGOSS is designed to take advantage of existing monitoring systems through the systematic collection, processing, and dissemination of oceanographic data. Phase I of IGOSS focuses on physical observations that are already routinely measured. The overall IGOSS Plan includes observations of chemical and biological variables whose interpretation depends on the prior collection of information on physical conditions, including atmospheric conditions near the interface.[12]

Because of budget and personnel restraints, IOC has been limited to a planning and coordinating organization with no real substantive or creative powers. The secretariat, composed of ten professionals and ten general service personnel in 1970, had an annual basic budget fund of only $241,000 and received another $491,000 from United Nations Development Program (UNDP) Technical Assistance. IOC membership is free, which may account for the comparatively large membership (approximately 70 states).

Unless this funding and personnel situation is drastically changed, IOC will probably remain a coordinating organization that helps scientists to get their work done, provides services to marine science through some world data centers, and supplies teaching or mutual assistance to developing countries. The early implementation of LEPOR (even expanded) and the GIPME is unlikely under present conditions. However, substantive success would be forthcoming through the use of established systems within the IGOSS program.

INTER-GOVERNMENTAL MARITIME
CONSULTATIVE ORGANIZATION

In 1948, the United Nations Geneva Maritime Conference drafted a convention to create an organization covering the whole field of sea transport and to provide a means for cooperation among governments on technical matters affecting international merchant shipping, with special emphasis on the safety of life at sea.[13] The convention received sufficient signatures to establish the International Maritime Consultative Organization (IMCO) formally by March 17, 1959. The first IMCO assembly met in London on January 6, 1959.

Before final establishment it had been agreed that IMCO would assume the depository function and other duties relating to the International Convention for the Prevention of Pollution of the Sea by Oil, 1954 (which had been temporarily undertaken by the United Kingdom), as well as United Nations responsibility for collecting and disseminating technical information about oil pollution. In preparation for the 1962 international conference on the prevention of pollution of the sea by oil, IMCO engaged in a worldwide survey on the extent of marine pollution by oil, the availability of ports for the reception of oil residues from ships, and the progress of research on other ways of combatting oil pollution. Based on this survey the 1962 conference agreed upon more stringent amendments that widened the scope of the 1954 agreement. These came into force on June 27, 1967 (see Chapter 2 for details). In 1965 the Subcommittee on Oil Pollution (later renamed the Subcommittee on Marine Pollution) was established within IMCO to keep the problem under review.[14]

The Torrey Canyon disaster of 1967 prompted IMCO to launch an 18-point program covering the legal and technical aspects of marine pollution. The IMCO assembly approved many of these recommendations including a call for improved national and regional cooperation, effective systems for reporting significant spillages of oil, and improvements in the application of the detection and enforcement clauses of the 1962 amendments. In October 1969 the sixth IMCO assembly approved further extensive amendments to the Oil Pollution Convention and its annexes. It also decided to convene a 1973 international conference on marine pollution to prepare an international agreement on restraining the contamination of the marine environment by vessels or other equipment.

IMCO convened an international legal conference in Brussels in November 1969 to examine possible changes in general maritime law whose need was illustrated by Torrey Canyon. The conference adopted and opened for signature the International Convention Relating to Intervention on High Seas in Cases of Oil Pollution Casualties (Public Law Convention) and the International Convention of Civil Liability for Oil Pollution Damage (Private Law Convention). The conference also established a working group on an international compensation fund for oil pollution damage, which reported to the IMCO legal committee on September 30, 1970.[15] An international legal conference was held in December 1971 to adopt a convention establishing an international compensation fund for oil pollution damage, and an extensive conference on other types of vessel-related pollution was held in 1973.

IMCO cooperates with other international organizations in the area of marine pollution. It is a joint sponsor of GESAMP, participates in activities related to the implementation of LEPOR, actively participated in the planning and preparations for the United Nations Human Environment Conference, and has been represented on the UN Committee on the Peaceful Uses of the Sea-Bed.

FOOD AND AGRICULTURAL ORGANIZATION

The FAO's fisheries department has been active in promoting the development of world fisheries. Its marine pollution activities have focused on promoting scientific information, such as abstracting services, for organizations within and outside the United Nations family.[16] The FAO Advisory Committee on Marine Resources Research (ACMRR) was involved in preparing the groundwork for the IOC working group on marine pollution, whose report laid the base for the comprehensive outline for LEPOR, and in the formation of GESAMP. FAO staff participated in a WHO training course on coastal pollution control in 1970, assisted IAEA with advice on the disposal of radioactive wastes in estuarine environments, and provided extensive information on the extent and effects of marine pollution on commercial fisheries to regional councils and commissions under its Committee on Fisheries (COFI).* Its

---

*At its tenth session in Rome, the General Fisheries Council for the Mediterranean adopted resolutions to implement the knowledge of the present status of marine

nongovernmental contacts include the International Association for Water Pollution Research (IAWPR), the International Association of Microbiological Societies (IAMS), and the International Law Association Committee on International Water Resource Law.

One of FAO's most significant activities was organization of the 1970 technical conference on marine pollution and its effects on living resources and fishing, which assembled an unprecedented number of experts to discuss every aspect of marine pollution and its influence on the living resources of the oceans.[17] The conference recognized marine pollution "to be part of the overall problem of the pollution of the human environment" and recommended "urgent action to prevent and combat pollution on international, regional, national and individual levels in order to minimize effects on the marine environment, its living resources and fishing."[18] To achieve this end the conference further recommended:

1. That the deliberate dumping of toxic and solid wastes on recognized and potential fishing grounds and other shallow water areas be prohibited.

2. That governments require all factories producing mercurial products or using mercury or its compounds as catalysts, cathodes or for other production purposes to adopt advanced techniques for mercury recovery, and that mercurial compounds used for agricultural or antigrowth purposes be replaced at the earliest possible time by other nonmercurial substitutes.

3. That research be increased on the effects of oil and aromatic hydrocarbons, and on ecologically less harmful substitutes for the persistent pesticides.

4. That pilot regional monitoring exercises, such as are being organized by the International Council for the Exploration of the Sea (ICES) for the North and Baltic seas, be undertaken as part of a preliminary exploratory survey for evaluation of the state of pollution of the world ocean.

5. That studies be undertaken to identify integrated ecological regions with a view to future promotion of regional marine pollution control agreements.

---

pollution in the Mediterranean and to urge governments to support the work of pollution experts nominated by member governments. A working party was established jointly with the ICSE of the Mediterranean ICSEM.

6. That a working group of lawyers, marine scientists, and other specialists be established to consider means for the regulation of the introduction into the marine environment of the most toxic and/or highly persistent pollutants.[19]

Although participants were somewhat restricted by the definition of the conference from going too far into general pollution problems, where possible they pursued the implications of marine pollution into related fields of control and prevention.

WORLD METEOROLOGICAL ORGANIZATION

While not primarily concerned with control of ocean pollution, WMO is the major UN specialized agency involved in research and monitoring of meteorological factors affecting the marine environment. WMO's major function is to promote the collection, processing, and analysis of data, as well as the standardization of instruments and techniques in hydrology through its commissions for hydrometeorology, oceanography, and climatology. In the collection of meteorological data, WMO has provided invaluable information on the atmosphere as a pathway to the ocean for organic and inorganic products released in the air or picked up from the ground by the wind.

WMO's executive committee has stressed the need for approaching the marine environment problem in the broad context of environmental pollution, an approach confirmed by the Seminar on the Methods of Detection Measurement and Monitoring of Pollutants in the Marine Environment, which endorsed the concept of the indivisible environment. It has been proposed that WMO's well-established international system for monitoring and predicting environmental conditions at the sea-air interface might be mobilized in support of marine pollution studies; monitoring and operations to combat oil spills could include ocean weather stations in the Atlantic and Pacific oceans and observation ships registered under the WMO selected ships scheme, complemented by the WMO system for monitoring background air pollution over land. This proposal led to the GESAMP recommendation of GIPME, on which WMO, through its advisory body to IOC, has been invited to cooperate and consider the best ways it can contribute.

WMO has already provided a number of meteorological services for operations to combat oil spills. Theoretical studies to improve the prediction of movement and dispersion of surface-drifting pollutants also have been carried out.

INTERNATIONAL ATOMIC ENERGY AGENCY

IAEA was established on July 29, 1957, on the basis of a statute approved on October 26, 1956 at an international conference held at United Nations headquarters.[20] By that statute IAEA was given responsibility for establishing standards of safety relating to the peaceful uses of nuclear energy and the management and disposal of resultant radioactive waste. Its statutory concern about possible pollution from the disposal of radioactive wastes in the sea was reinforced by the 1958 United Nations Conference on the Law of the Sea, which recommended that IAEA pursue studies to help control such disposals by drawing up internationally acceptable preventive regulations.[21] Major roles in the IAEA's efforts to cope with environmental radiation hazards are played by the IAEA's division of life science (including sections on radiation biology, nuclear medicine, and dosimetry); the joint FAO/IAEA division of atomic energy in food and agriculture; its divisions of health, safety and waste disposal, and research and laboratories; and the IAEA's laboratories at Monaco, Seibersdorf, and headquarters (Vienna).*

IAEA requires that a wide range of health and safety rules be applied to its own activities and to any project it assists. These rules cover all peaceful uses of nuclear energy from the safe handling of radioisotopes in small laboratories to the safe operation of large nuclear power plants. They are periodically revised to take account of new technological developments, scientific knowledge, and practical experience.[22]

In November 1970 IAEA convened a panel on procedures for establishing limits for radionuclides in the sea, to

----

*Initially, the Monaco laboratory concentrated on basic research on physical, chemical, and biological problems relating to marine activity. Its program has evolved away from this orientation toward standardizating and coordinating reference and analytical techniques used in marine radioactivity studies, evaluating scientific information needed to assess hazards, and collaboration and assistance with member states on request.

consider methods for determining critical nuclides and
their movement through the marine food web to various
sectors of the population that use marine food. It also
reviewed the programs of investigation required to facilitate this identification procedure.[23] The panel issued
a report entitled "Principles for Limiting the Introduction of Radioactive Waste into the Sea," under the sponsorship of IAEA and WHO, presenting basic principles concerning the marine disposal of radioactive wastes and
their practical application.[24]

One of the proposals IAEA has considered is the establishment of a registry for radioactive materials disposed at sea by member states, to be linked to a more
comprehensive international registry of other ocean pollutants. Progress toward this goal has been hindered by
the insistence of certain members, notably the USSR, that
no radioactive waste materials should be disposed at sea.
National security considerations complicate the willingness of the United States to participate in any registry
that would include the military use and disposal of nuclear wastes.

IAEA has collaborated successfully with other organizations on joint fields of interest. WHO, for example, has adopted many of IAEA's safety publications for
recommendation to national health authorities, and has
issued many rules under joint sponsorship with IAEA.
Nearly all international transport bodies--such as the
IMCO, the International Aviation Transport Association,
and the Railway, Road and Inland Waterway Organization of
Europe--have incorporated IAEA regulation for the safe
transport of radioactive materials. Through its joint
division of atomic energy in food and agriculture, IAEA
has investigated the use of radioisotopes and radiation
in studies dealing with pesticides and their residues.
It convened a panel of experts in October 1970 from other
UN specialized agencies to advise on priorities, research,
information needs, and steps to be taken to assist the
development of effective pest control techniques.[25] The
Joint Division has also been assigned responsibility for
collecting information on the contamination of goods and
the agricultural environment by radionuclides derived
from accidental or intentional releases into the biosphere.

WORLD HEALTH ORGANIZATION

WHO environmental health research activities include
such issues as the disposal of waste in offshore waters,

116

general coastal pollution, and health aspects of sea food products. Its work in these areas falls into four main categories: assistance to member and especially developing countries, research and training activities, the establishment of relevant reference and documentation centers, and cooperation with other agencies. As part of its environmental pollution control program, WHO activities include comparative studies in water pollution legislation,[26] problems related to waste disposal from ships in harbors, and ship sanitation in general. Supported by the UNDP, WHO has been carrying out a number of field projects on waste disposal and the development of public health staff to deal with coastal pollution control in Ceylon, Taiwan, Ghana, Ivory Coast, Morocco, the Philippines, Senegal, and Turkey.[27] The goal of these projects is to avoid serious public health problems by developing immediate and long-term multistage programs for the controlled collection, treatment, and disposal of domestic and industrial wastes into coastal waters. WHO also maintains educational programs in sanitary engineering, waste treatment, and disposal into fresh water and marine environment (for example, the 1970-71 Inter-regional Training Course in Coastal Water Pollution held in Denmark).

WHO has established an International Reference Center on Waste Disposal to develop research programs relating to the storage, collection, treatment, reuse, and ultimate disposal of liquid and solid wastes; an International Reference Center on Water Quality Monitoring to promote uniform water quality assessment methodology; and an International Reference Center on Marine Biotoxins to assess the hazards of natural toxins and manmade pollutants on marine life. All three reference centers are intended to develop a yet unrecognized universal basis for establishing the maximum microbial counts above which a danger of infection exists. Such a foundation would be instrumental in the drafting of international legislation regarding the quality of coastal water with respect to microbiological contamination and chemical pollution.[28]

WHO also conducts studies on the effects of pesticides on human health, advises on protective measures, and defines standards. It has established international reference centers on vector biology and on the toxicology of pesticides. The WHO/FAO Codex Alimentarius Commission is a principal forum for discussing and recommending allowable residues in food.

JOINT GROUP OF EXPERTS ON THE SCIENTIFIC
ASPECTS OF MARINE POLLUTION

Following consideration by the Administrative Committee on Coordination of UN organizations and subsidiary
bodies, a number of agencies agreed in 1967 to establish
a joint group of experts to advise them on scientific
aspects of marine pollution. The establishment of the
joint group (GESAMP), open to sponsorship by any organization of the UN system, was intended "to encourage the
various organizations concerned at their discretion to
disband or to refrain from establishing other interdisciplinary groups on the subject and so avoid duplication of efforts."[29]

GESAMP held its first session in March 1969, sponsored by only four agencies: IMCO, FAO, UNESCO, and WMO.
By its fourth session in March 1972, these agencies had
been joined by WHO, IAEA, and the UN proper. Sponsoring
organizations agree in principle on a slate of members,
appointed by each in its individual capacity, and accept
responsibility for contacts with and expenses of the members they nominate. The group meets annually for approximately one week; members work on specific problems assigned to them during intersessional periods. IMCO as-
signs an administrative secretary responsible for maintaining continuity in GESAMP's work; each sponsoring
organization designates a technical secretary responsible
for the preparation of the report when it acts as host
for a session.

GESAMP advises the sponsoring organizations and the
IOC on the scientific aspects of marine pollution and
assists IOC and UN organizations concerned in the development of LEPOR. It advises on matters relating to the establishment of effective exchange arrangements and on the
scientific aspects of the needs and criteria for inter-
governmental instruments for the control of marine pollution. It also assists in the preparation of relevant
technical conferences, considers specific questions put
to it by sponsoring agencies, and provides advice on particular problems to any member state requesting it through
a sponsoring organization.

At its first session GESAMP discussed the need for
scientific research on particular problems associated
with marine pollution, particularly the use and effects
of chemical absorbants and dispersants.[30] It reviewed
research priorities with a view toward facilitating international action for pollution control, examined the effects

of various pollutants on marine flora and fauna, and determined the permissible concentration of some pollutants. The second session focused on the scientific basis for a marine pollution monitoring system and registration of discharges; it also reviewed the FAO technical conference on marine pollution.[31] The third session prepared a review of harmful chemical substances, identified noxious and hazardous cargoes, and examined the health aspects of marine pollution in terms of microbiological pollutants, toxicological problems, and the technical and scientific aspects of coastal pollution control.[32] It also discussed marine pollution problems in relation to LEPOR. The fourth session elaborated on the review of harmful chemical substances presented at the third session and examined predischarge treatment technologies for certain pollutants. It also reviewed the report of the first meeting of IOC's GELTSPAP and its recommendations for the development of the Global Investigation of Pollution in the Marine Environment (GIPME) and other related LEPOR matters.

NORTH ATLANTIC TREATY ORGANIZATION

In November 1969 the North Atlantic Council (NATO's governing body) established a Committee on the Challenges of Modern Society (CCMS) as a regular Council committee, chaired by the secretary general of NATO or his representative, to "consider specific problems of the human environment with the deliberate objective of stimulating action by member governments.[33] CCMS chose as one of its first and most urgently needed pilot projects the study of pollution of coastal waters, with Belgium as the pilot and Canada, France, and Portugal as copilot countries. As the first program in the project, the Belgian government held a colloquium on pollution of the sea by oil spills, in cooperation with the United States, at NATO headquarters in Brussels on November 2-6, 1970.

The colloquium had a twofold purpose: (1) to take stock of the existing state of knowledge concerning the dangers of oil spills and (2) on that basis, to recommend practical action for solving the many connected problems.[34] For the Atlantic international community, the colloquium represented the first test of NATO's resolve to confront environmental problems and of its ability to adapt its traditional mutual defense system to a new orientation. For the world community, it indicated the resolve of developed countries to restrict their technologies and pay higher costs for a clean environment.

John Volpe, (then) U.S. transportation secretary, told the colloquium that it had the opportunity to demonstrate "responsible leadership that will be clearly recognized around the world, to recommend actions that will sharpen the focus of international action attention, and to work a catalytic effect on international progress in this field."[35] To achieve these ends, Volpe recommended that NATO identify and recommend action to set the international community on a course leading to the solution of the global ocean oil spills problem, including a complete halt on all international discharges of oil and oily waste into the oceans by tankers and other vessels by 1975; accelerated research into the effects and prevention of oil spills; improved ship construction standards; and preparation of national and international plans for coping with spill contingencies.[36]

Other delegates, notably the United Kingdom, were less enthusiastic about the new NATO role proposed by the United States. One United Kingdom delegate noted the value of information exchange but stressed his government's belief that it was neither "desirable or necessary to set up additional continuing organizations which might detract from the efforts which governments are putting into solution . . . through existing channels."[37] He urged that existing IMCO conventions be enforced, that the load-on-top (LOT) technique be universally adopted, and that oil-water separators be improved.

Still others expressed the belief that the target date of 1975 was unrealistic, and that the time required for altering tanker designs to incorporate recent developments for clean ballast operations (including LOT) was too short. These delegates also predicted that there would not be enough shore reception facilities for LOT wastes by 1975.

The colloquium modified the U.S. proposal to accommodate these views. The NATO Council resolved "to start work at once in order to achieve by 1975, if possible, but not later than the end of the decade, the elimination of intentional discharges of oil and oily wastes into the sea." [Emphasis added.][38]

Pilot project activity has been limited since the colloquium. NATO's environmental role has generally been deferred until the results of the Stockholm Conference have been assessed.

ECONOMIC COMMISSION FOR EUROPE

Environmental activities carried out within the ECE include regional water pollution studies. Water resource utilization surveys, reviews, analyses, and forecasts are handled by the ECE Committee on Water Problems Within its Environment and Housing Division. This committee is also responsible for selected problems of water pollution control and various projects on the formulation and administration of water management plans.[39]

As part of the UN Economic and Social Council, ECE includes the principal technologically advanced countries and, consequently, an area where environmental concern is strongest. Its May 1971 Conference on Environment at Prague was most significant in its policy and action orientation and through its convenience as a forum for the systematic exchange of experience. Although marine pollution was not one of the specific topics discussed at the Prague Conference, important information regarding the coordination of governmental policies on water pollution control was discussed.

International cooperation in the field of water pollution control, a 1970 ECE survey stated, takes place bilaterally by virtue of numerous agreements on the utilization of common boundary waters.[40] These agreements have been concluded between all European boundary waters of economic significance, and between the United States, Canada, and Mexico. Multilateral agreements in the field of water pollution control have led to the establishment of the following bodies: the International Commission for the Protection of the Rhine against Pollution (West Germany, France, Luxembourg, the Netherlands, Switzerland); International Commission for the Protection of the Waters of Lake Constance (Austria, West Germany, Switzerland); the Permanent Tripartite Commission on Polluted Waters (Belgium, France, Luxembourg); and the International Commission for the Protection of the Mosel and the Saar against Pollution (West Germany, France, Luxembourg). The functional experience of these commissions was discussed at the ECE meeting.

In preparation for the Prague Conference, ECE held a meeting of senior government advisers on environment in Geneva from November 30 to December 3, 1970. The meeting considered some of the principal issues on which government policies might concentrate including: (1) how to develop environmental standards and regulations concerning

the allocation and manner of use of natural resources;
(2) how to establish pricing, taxing, and subsidizing
policies in support of environmental objectives; (3) how
to set comprehensive and systematic fiscal priorities
aimed at improving the environment; (4) whether to put
more emphasis on preventive measures; and (5) how to har-
monize policies internationally by means of bilateral,
subregional, and regional cooperation and agreements.[41]
The meeting provided much information on the methods of
decision-making and the problems, but little was discussed
in relation to specific measures or actions that ought to
be undertaken.[42]

ECE work priorities have included a 1972 seminar to
discuss the final draft of a manual for the compilation
of balances of water resources and needs; the organization
of a study tour to visit automatic water quality monitoring stations; a seminar on the economics of water management; and studies on optimization of investment choices.

ORGANIZATION FOR ECONOMIC COOPERATION
AND DEVELOPMENT

OECD's continuing work on the unintended occurrence
of pesticide residues considers their concentration in
the marine food chain. Its Water Management Research
Group (WMRG) is primarily concerned with fresh water
bodies but is somewhat involved in research on waterborne
contaminants in estuaries. Under OECD's auspices, the
European Nuclear Energy Agency (ENEA) deposited low-level
solid radioactive wastes in ocean waters off the coast of
Portugal in 1967 and Ireland in 1969.

INTERNATIONAL COUNCIL FOR SCIENTIFIC UNIONS

The ICSU Scientific Committee on Oceanic Research
(SCOR) promotes international oceanic research cooperation
and arranges such international conferences as the Joint
Oceanic Assembly. ICSU plans to do research on ocean
pollution problems through its scientific Committee on
Problems of the Environment (SCOPE).

INTERNATIONAL COUNCIL FOR EXPLORATION OF THE SEA

ICES coordinates oceanographic activities in the
North Atlantic and adjacent seas. It coordinates the

activities of member governments and other interested
bodies, promotes research in the marine sciences, and
seeks to establish the best basis for international conventions on the improvement of sea fisheries. It cooperates with the FAO, UNESCO, and other international organizations specializing in the marine sciences.

CONCLUSION

The evolution of concern for marine pollution within
the United Nations family and the establishment of such
interagency forums as GESAMP and the intergovernmental
working group on marine pollution for the Stockholm Conference indicates a general recognition of the need for a
coordinated interdisciplinary approach. But no single
specialized agency has sufficient funds to assume the expense required for such a broad undertaking. The most
successful agency in promoting international marine pollution agreements operates at a funding level of about $1
million per year, making it one of the most poorly financed organizations of the United Nations.[43]
The tendency of each organization to look at the
problem from its own perspective has complicated and im-
peded effective international control over all pollutants.
IMCO's bias toward major shipping and transportation industries limits its usefulness as an effective forum for
strict controls; historically, its agreements have been
largely limited to confirming what the transportation industry has already found to be economically and opera-
tionally acceptable. IAEA cannot enforce safe methods of
operation or disposal except in activities it sponsors or
to which it provides fissionable material. The Soviet
insistence that no sea disposal take place militates
against IAEA agreement on controlling the disposal of
radioactive waste at sea. WHO and FAO face the DDT dilemma,
recognizing its environmental hazards on the one hand but
continuing to advocate its agricultural and public health
uses for want of economical substitutes. One WHO report
has even stated that "modern man cannot do without pesticides and detergents."[44] While organizational contradic-
tions have been minimized in interagency efforts, they
often engender the plodding pace and cautious language,
characteristic of GESAMP reports.
All the specialized agencies of the UN system and
GESAMP serve as advisory and research coordinating systems;
limited budgets and small staffs prohibit them from going
beyond these capacities. The infrequent coordinating

efforts, while important, do not provide the quick comprehensive overview necessary to provide decision-makers with the clearcut and needed alternatives that now exist. Any movement to increase GESAMP's scope and authority (especially to permanently link it with decision-making mechanisms) increases rational policy and decreases political irresponsibility. Environmental policy-making is only as good as its primary scientific information system.

Organizations outside the UN system, notably the Committee on the Challenges of Modern Society (CCMS) and the Organization for Economic Cooperation and Development (OECD), can play important roles in achieving better management of the oceans. The European Economic Community and the UN Economic Commission for Europe perform important functions in the development of standard regulations, in eliminating counterproductive economic competition, and in providing economic incentives for maintaining strict controls. Integrated river basin management, a target of ECE programs, will eventually provide uniform discharge limits for multinational rivers.

NATO possesses the potential of a leadership role as a model of regional agreement. The stumbling block of evolving from a purely politicomilitary alliance system diminishes with détente. The adoption of an Atlantic Convention on the Prevention of Marine Pollution, binding members through parallel national legislation to policies and guidelines already agreed upon through IMCO but stalled awaiting ratification by all IMCO members, would establish NATO's leadership role. The first serious multilateral attempt to enforce regulations limiting marine pollution could be instituted by the development of contingency plans (a function familiar to NATO and most military command structures) for coping with massive oil and other pollutant spills and an enforcement-surveillance system based on NATO ships.

However, from an institutional perspective, international cooperation on problems of the marine environment will probably be achieved best within the framework of the United Nations. The main forum for debating the issues and ultimately for agreeing upon measures for controlling ocean pollution must include nations with substantial oceanographic capabilities, large maritime fleets, and coastal industrial potential. It must be able to deal with global monitoring schemes, broad-based research on climatological problems, and assistance to developing countries by increasing the amount of food from the sea and developing the rational exploitation of seabed mineral resources. Only a combination of the United Nations and its specialized agencies can fulfill such a wide range of necessary functions.

International cooperative efforts are only as strong and effective as the political will of the participants. No combination of organizations, UN or otherwise, can adopt or enact regulatory schemes without the active endorsement of a majority, and in some cases the unanimity, of the membership. Organizational structures serve essentially as tools, not rigid vehicles, for international cooperation. Different tools can be used to achieve different functions; if basic agreement on courses of action can be reached, the international organizational structure is flexible enough to adapt to the needs. The proliferation of organizations, proposals, and their attendant maze of alphabet soup acronyms does not represent general international confusion; it is a symptom of the lack of political will and the inability of the sovereign nation-state system to adapt to today's needs. If governments were serious about international environmental reform and genuinely recognized the long-term hazards of marine pollution, they would choose an organization and use it. By debating basically the same topics and arriving at the same conclusions year after year, governments have maintained the illusion of serious negotiation when in fact they have done little. The 1972 GESAMP meeting discussed many of the same unresolved issues as Prince Ranier's 1965 Monaco report to IOC. NATO has enlarged upon IMCO while FAO has accomplished much that was intended for IOC's LEPOR. IOC in turn proposed GIPME and GELTSPAP, while WMO moved into the environmental arena with IGOSS and other monitoring proposals.

The international organizations cannot be blamed for the confusion; they have only done what has been expected of them. The first sign of serious cooperative efforts will be massive consolidation of old organizations or the establishment of new forums with comprehensive capability. Without one or the other, international environmental efforts are reducible to empty rhetoric and meaningless verbiage.

1. Report of the secretary general to United Nations Economic and Social Council, The Sea: Prevention and Control of Marine Pollution, UN DOC E/5003 (May 7, 1971), p. 67.

2. Sidney Holt, "A Biased History of the I.O.C.," in Proceedings of the Law of the Sea Institute (1970) (Kingston, R.I.: University of Rhode Island, 1970).

3. See Centre Scientifique de Monaco, Pollution of the Sea, Report of the Centre submitted to IOC, fourth session (Paris, November 3-12, 1965).

4. Centre Scientifique de Monaco, Report of the first meeting of the IOC Working Group on Marine Pollution (Paris: UNESCO, August 14-17, 1967), IOC DOC No. V-14/SC/CS/150, p. 1.

5. Ibid., pp. 1-3.

6. UNESCO-IOC, Report of the first IOC Working Group on Marine Pollution, op. cit.

7. See UNESCO-IOC, sixth session, Summary Report (Paris: UNESCO, September 2-13, 1969), SC/MD/19, pp. 12-13, Res. VI-15.

8. Ibid., Annex IV. For draft, see SC/IOC-VI/7 App.

9. Ibid.

10. Ibid., Part 1, Sec. 3, pp. 12-13.

11. Ibid., p. 13.

12. UNCAM-Inter-Governmental Working Group on Monitoring and Surveillance, Report of the first session (Geneva, August 27, 1971), UN DOC A/Conf. 48/IWGM.I/3, p. 16.

13. IMCO secretariat, "Activities of the IMCO in Relation to Marine Pollution" (London, July 25, 1970).

14. L. Leplat, "IMCO Combats Marine Pollution," Marine Pollution Bulletin 1, no. 8 (August 1971): 124.

15. IMCO Working Group on International Convention on the Fund for Oil Pollution Damage, Report of the Legal Committee on Legislation, WG/(FUND) II/4 (London, IMCO HQ: mimeo.; September 30, 1970).

16. See, for example, the new FAO Journal, Aquatic Biology, and Fisheries Abstracts and List of Experts on Marine Pollution (Rome: FAO, 1970 Technical Conference on Marine Pollution Paper, 1970).

17. Report of the FAO Conference on Marine Pollution (Rome, 1971).

18. Ibid. See also "Conclusions and Recommendations as Approved," in Report of FAO Technical Conference on Marine Pollution, FIR:MP/70/Rec., Rome, FAO: Rev 1 (February 17, 1971), p. 1.

19. Report of the FAO Technical Conference, op. cit. (1971).

20. UN Office of Public Information, Basic Facts About the UN (New York, 1970), p. 64.

21. The Sea, op. cit., p. 73.

22. U.S. Department of State, Committee on International Environmental Affairs: Task Force III, "U.S. Priority Interests in the Environment Activities of International organizations" (Washington, D.C., December 1970), p. 11.

23. The Sea, op. cit., p. 74.

24. IAEA/WHO, "Principles for Limiting the Introduction of Radioactive Waste into the Sea" (Vienna: IAEA, 1971).

25. "U.S. Priority Interests," op. cit., pp. 103-4.

26. WHO, Control of Water Pollution: A Survey of Existing Legislation (Geneva: WHO, 1967).

27. The Sea, op. cit., p. 72.

28. Ibid.

29. Administrative Secretariat at IMCO, "Updated Memorandum" on the Joint GESAMP, GESAMP III/2 (London: January 11, 1971).

30. GESAMP I/11, July 17, 1969 (London, first session, March 17-21, 1969).

31. GESAMP II/11, June 20, 1970 (Paris: UNESCO, March 2-6, 1970).

32. GESAMP III/19, May 13, 1971 (Rome: FAO, February 22-27, 1971). See also GESAMP/37 (London, IMCO: January 29, 1971) "Questionnaire on Pollution of the Marine Environment," submitted by IMCO.

33. NATO Committee on the Challenges of Modern Society, Coastal Water Pollution, Pollution of the Sea by Oil Spills; Report of the Colloquium, No. 1 (Brussels: NATO, 1970), p. 146.

34. Ibid.

35. Ibid., p. 21.

36. Ibid. See remarks and address of John Volpe, U.S. secretary of transportation.

37. Ibid., p. 26.

38. Ibid., p. 27.

39. Economic Commission for Europe, "Draft Program of Action by the ECE in the Field of Environment," Environmental Working Paper No. 5 (Geneva: ECE, 1971, mimeo), p. 7.

40. Economic Commission for Europe, Trends in Water Resources Use and Development, Doc. No. ST/ECE/WATER (Geneva: 1970).

41. Economic Commission for Europe/ENV/2, p. 8;
"Report of the Meeting of Senior Government Advisors on
Environment" (Geneva: December 15, 1970, mimeo).
42. Note by the Secretariat of the ECE Meeting of
Senior Governmental Advisors on Environment, "Identification of Information Needed to Promote Strong and Workable
Environmental Action on National and International Scales,"
Environmental Working Paper No. 4 (Geneva: August 25,
1970).
43. Max Edwards, "Oil Pollution and the Law," in
Stanley Degler, ed., Oil Pollution (Washington, D.C.:
Bureau of National Affairs, 1969), p. 27.
44. P. Macuch, "The Problems and Prospects of Environmental Pollution Control in Europe: Commentary on
the Long-Term Progress of Environmental Pollution Control
of the WHO Regional Office for Europe" (Prague: Charles
University, October 13-15, 1969).

International approaches to the control of marine
pollution will be governed in large part by the forums in
which they are discussed. Each forum is limited in its
own way. One may be too comprehensive in its scope, too
all-encompassing in its proposals, and consequently too
vague and general in its conclusions. Another may be circumscribed from the beginning as to the topics, pollutants,
or pollutant sources it may consider; proposals generated
in such contexts may be of limited effect. And a third,
possessing unquestionable competence and authority, may
be preoccupied with other law of the sea issues and so
may place less emphasis on problems of environmental quality.
Three international forums have emerged which possess
both the willingness and competence to conclude global and
regional agreements on the control of marine pollution:
The United Nations Conference of the Human Environment
(June 1972, Stockholm); The Inter-Governmental Maritime
Consultative Organization Conference on Marine Pollution
(1973, London); and the United Nations Committee on the
Peaceful Uses of the Sea-Bed-Law of the Sea Conference
(proposed for 1973-74). The preparations and proposals
for these conferences provide an indication of the kinds
of agreements that may emanate from similar future forums.

UNITED NATIONS CONFERENCE ON THE HUMAN ENVIRONMENT

In February 1971 the preparatory committee for the
UN Conference on the Human Environment heard presentations
on the various marine pollution activities of the United

Nations system and discussed the problems of promoting effective measures for prevention and control. In light of
the "urgency, importance and complexity" of the problem,
the committee established an intergovernmental working
group to "look at the problem of marine pollution as a
whole and attempt to develop an integrated plan for dealing with marine pollution."[1] The plan was intended to
take into account areas in which the UN system was already
active as well as those in which new initiatives were
needed.

There was some discussion of whether specific action
to control marine pollution should be taken at the Stockholm Conference. Some delegations stated that they would
like to see the deliberate dumping of toxic materials and
the discharge of chlorinated hydrocarbons into the marine
environment dealt with.[2] Others felt such actions need
not take the form of conventions.[3] A working group was
established to consider and recommend specific actions.
If the working group found that agreement on specific action on marine pollution should be left to the IMCO Vessel
Pollution Conference or the Law of the Sea Conference, it
was agreed that the Stockholm Conference would only consider general plans and recommended guidelines. The preparatory committee further recognized that "many significant sources of marine pollution are totally unrelated to
marine activities and therefore may not be taken under
consideration by either the forthcoming Conference on the
Law of the Sea or IMCO."[4] It cited as examples pollutants
that reach the sea directly from the land or the atmosphere.

The conference secretariat cautiously suggested final
actions on specific aspects of marine pollution that might
be taken at Stockholm and that were, in its judgment,
"both urgent and feasible."[5] It cited debate in the preceding General Assembly Session in which a number of
states had said that final action on ocean dumping should
be taken at Stockholm. Then the secretariat added: "But
it is for Governments to decide not only what particular
activity or source of pollutants they wish to bring under
control, such as ocean dumping, but also the nature of
the action they wish to prepare for [Level III] action
level preparations."[6] Other specific recommendations on
marine pollution deemed possibilities for action at Stockholm included a monitoring system, intensified research
under the Long-Term and Expanded Program of Oceanic Exploration and Research (LEPOR), and a "voluntarily" submitted information registry of discharges and spillages

of certain specified pollutants.[7] Finally, the secretariat suggested that states could agree at Stockholm, as at other UN conferences, on a "statement of principles which, while perhaps not taking the force of law, would serve the useful purpose of laying down guidelines which States might be expected to respect during the period in which negotiations went forward on specific conventions which would have legal force."[8]

In its charge to the working group, the preparatory committee noted these suggestions and asked further that the group recommend:

1. General guidelines and criteria to assist governments in preventing or controlling marine pollution;
2. Specific actions required for:
   (a) those substances which, because of their toxicity, persistence, accumulation in living tissues or other properties, should be prevented or limited;
   (b) regional or subregional arrangements to give immediate protection to areas of the marine environment which are especially liable to dangerous pollution;
   (c) improved enforcement by Governments of existing instruments or conventions relating to the prevention and control of marine pollution and the early implementation of further instruments.[9]

The first session of the Inter-Governmental Working Group on Marine Pollution (IWGMP) was held in June 1971 at IMCO headquarters under the sponsorship of the United Kingdom and was attended by representatives of 38 UN member states together with representatives of FAO, IAEA, WHO, UNESCO, and IMCO. At its first meeting the working group confirmed specific actions that should be prepared for the Stockholm Conference:

1. _Ocean dumping._ The participants agreed to study a draft convention on the regulations of transportation for ocean dumping submitted by the United States.

2. _Regional cooperation._ Participants urged states bordering enclosed or semi-enclosed seas to take steps during the intersessional period to develop regional

arrangements to deal with common marine pollution problems. They also requested the parties to the negotiations
on the proposed arrangements for the North and Mediterranean seas to present progress reports.

    3. <u>National regulation guidelines</u>. Members experi-
enced in the regulation of marine pollution were requested
to submit papers on national legislation to enable the
group to formulate general guidelines.

    4. <u>Rank order of pollutants</u>. Comments were invited
on recent GESAMP findings.

    5. <u>Monitoring</u>. The group recommended that sources
of significant pollutants be identified.

    6. <u>Developing country participation</u>. The group
agreed to consider means of assuring maximum participation of developing countries in future deliberations.[10]

    IWGMP held its second session in Ottawa, Canada, in
November 1971, this time attended by 42 UN member states
and the usual UN specialized agency representatives. Two
working parties were established to consider general guidelines and principles, and to draft conventions on ocean
dumping.

    Following the preliminary debates based in large part
on papers submitted by Canada, the United Kingdom, Spain,
and the secretariat, the working party identified and formulated a series of guiding concepts as a basis for general agreement. These concepts included a definition of
marine pollution, a statement of objectives, and a list
of principles for the preservation of the marine environment. These included:

        1. That the marine environment and all
the living organisms it supports are
vital to humanity.

        2. That the capacity of the sea to assim-
ilate wastes and to regenerate natural
resources is not unlimited.

        3. That states should use the best prac-
ticable means available to them to
minimize the discharge of potentially
hazardous substances to the sea by all
routes, including land-based sources
such as rivers, outfalls, and pipelines within national jurisdiction.

        4. That states should assume joint re-
sponsibility for the preservation of
the marine environment beyond the limits of national jurisdiction, and when

appropriate should join together in concerted policies and common measures to
prevent the pollution of areas which form
natural or integrated entities for geo-
graphical or ecological reasons.[11]

The Canadian delegation submitted three more restrictive proposals based on its Arctic waters pollution prevention legislation:

1. A state could exercise special authority in sea areas adjacent to its territorial waters "where functional controls of a continuing nature are necessary for the effective prevention of
pollution which could cause damage or
injury to the land or marine environment under its exclusive or sovereign
authority."
2. A coastal state could prohibit any vessel that did not comply with reasonable
national rules and standards from entering waters under its environmental
protection authority.
3. These rights or powers should be based,
in addition to the specific purpose
zone adjacent to territorial waters
concept, on a responsibility of the
coastal state to the international
community and humanity as a whole; and
they must be consistent with the
state's primary responsibility for
marine environmental protection in the
areas concerned, subject to international rules and standards and the review before an appropriate international tribunal.[12]

The working group responsible for drafting articles
on ocean dumping held five meetings. Under the provisions
of the articles it approved, contracting parties would
pledge to take individual or collective measures to prevent marine pollution caused by the dumping of harmful
substances from ships, aircraft, or stationary platforms
at sea.[13] The dumping at sea of toxic mercury, cadmium,
organosilicon compounds, biological and chemical warfare
agents, (high-level) radioactive wastes, and oil and

derivative hydrocarbons other than those deemed biological-
ly harmless, would be forbidden except:

    1. In cases of <u>force majeure</u> when human lives or
safety of vessel (or property) is endangered.

    2. When such matter is present in low concentra-
tions in wastes whose dumping is allowed, provided that
these substances have not been added to the wastes in order to dump them at sea.[14]

States would have the power to issue dumping permits
for other matter, but none could be granted "if the dumping of matter or the continued dumping thereof would
(materially) endanger human health, welfare or amenities,
the marine environment, living and other marine resources,
ecological systems, or other legitimate uses of the sea."[15]
Special permits would be required for such substances as
radioactive wastes, arsenic, lead, copper and zinc and
their compounds, cyanides and fluorides, pesticides, and
other matter having equivalent effects.[16] Nothing in the
convention would prevent states, individually or jointly,
from establishing stricter criteria and prohibitions.[17]

Approval of the draft articles by the working group
was not regarded as binding, either as regards the terms
of particular articles or the form the provisions might
finally take. The working group stressed that formulation of the articles was not meant to prejudice the question of their eventual inclusion in a Stockholm convention,
recommendation, or draft resolution.

IMCO CONFERENCE ON MARINE POLLUTION

Noting the increased number of ships at sea and the
corresponding increase in the probability of accidents,
the growth in size of individual tankers, and the increasing diversity and quantity of petroleum derivatives and
other chemical cargoes carried by ships, the IMCO Assembly decided in October 1969 to convene an international
conference in 1974 "for the purpose of placing restraints
on the contamination of the sea, land and air by ships,
vessels or other equipment operating in the marine environment."[18] As a further step, in March 1971 the IMCO
Maritime Safety Committee approved a draft resolution in-
viting the assembly to decide:

        1. That the 1973 Conference shall have as
            its main objective, the achievement by
            1975 if possible, but certainly by the

end of the decade, the complete elimination of the willful and intentional pollution of the seas by oil and noxious
substances other than oil, and the mini-
mization of accidental spills;
2. That the Maritime Safety Committee
should direct its appropriate Sub-
Committee to give first priority to
the problem of achieving these goals.[19]

At its twenty-sixth session (June 7-10, 1971) the
IMCO Council decided that the following instruments and
related measures should be included in the agenda for
the conference if the 1975 target was to be achieved:

1. Revision of the International Convention for the Prevention of Pollution
of the Sea by Oil (1954) to provide
for the complete elimination of the
willful and intentional pollution of
the seas by oil.
2. Extension of the 1954 Convention or
the establishment of a new convention
to provide for the complete elimination of discharges caused by activities such as tank washing and bilge
discharge involving noxious and hazardous cargoes other than oil.[20]
3. Adjusting the Convention to minimize
accidental spillage of oil and other
noxious substances.
4. Establishment of an instrument dealing
with the safe carriage of dangerous
goods from the protection of the marine
environment point of view and revision
of the International Maritime Dangerous
Goods Code and the Code for the Construction and Equipment of Ships Carrying Dangerous Chemicals in Bulk.[21]
5. International standards or guidelines
for the disposal of ship-generated
garbage, sewage, and waste.

The IMCO Council also recommended that the conference establish schemes for the effective detection, reporting, and enforcement of existing or future conventions. Action, it concluded, might be directed toward

providing a uniform system for dealing with such offenses
and developing uniform penalties. The IMCO Council also
recommended considering a procedure for rapid amendment
of conventions to update standards and regulations in
keeping with the changing conditions of marine transportation.

The IMCO Council decided that the organization should
continue its work in certain other areas despite the fact
that they would be considered in the UN Conference on the
Human Environment and the Law of the Sea Conference.
These included:

1. Developing a new convention to regulate intentional or accidental pollution of the seas by oil and other substances from offshore facilities.
2. Establishing a new convention prohibit-
   ing the deliberate dumping by ships and
   barges of wastes containing certain
   persistent and very toxic pollutants
   especially those which may accumulate
   in biological materials.
3. The extension of the Brussels Conventions on Intervention and Civil Liability to cover pollution casualties by
   noxious and hazardous cargoes other
   than oil and those resulting from exploitation of the seabed and ocean
   floor.

UN COMMITTEE ON THE PEACEFUL USES
OF THE SEA-BED

In December 1970 the UN General Assembly enlarged to
86 members the former ad hoc Committee on the Peaceful
Uses of the Sea-Bed and instructed it to prepare a draft
treaty of articles embodying an equitable international
regime, including international machinery, for the area
and the resources of the seabed.[22] The draft articles
would be considered by an International Conference on the
Law of the Sea, which the General Assembly decided to convene in 1973.[23] In addition to its work on an international regime, the committee was instructed to prepare
draft articles on other subjects and issues related to
the law of the sea, including the preservation of the
marine environment.[24] The General Assembly also confirmed

the committee's original terms of reference (Resolution
2467 XXIII of December 21, 1968):

1. To study legal principles that would
   promote international cooperation in
   the exploration and use of the seabed
   and ocean floor beyond national jurisdiction.
2. To study ways of promoting the exploitation and use of the area's resources.
3. To examine measures to prevent maritime
   pollution [emphasis added].
4. To study the reservation of the international seabed for peaceful purposes,
   taking disarmament negotiations into
   account.[25]

The enlarged Sea-Bed Committee met in Geneva on
March 1-26, 1971. Following two weeks of informal con-
sultations the committee formed three subcommittees whose
subjects and functions were limited to items on which
there was agreement. Subcommittee I was assigned responsibility to prepare draft treaty articles embodying the
international regime, including international machinery;
Subcommittee II was assigned the preparation of a comprehensive list of subjects and issues related to the law of
the sea; Subcommittee III was delegated authority to
"deal with the preservation of the marine environment
(including the prevention of pollution) . . . and to prepare draft treaty articles thereon."[26]

Subcommittee III held its first meeting on March 25,
1971. The chairman, Mr. van dor Essen of Belgium, urged
the delegates to study the problems and proposals and to
prepare themselves for the July session of the Sea-Bed
Committee. John R. Stevenson of the United States expressed his delegation's conviction that marine pollution
and the preservation of the marine environment were appropriate subjects for international action and entered President Nixon's suggestions on essential measures to be taken
by the international community in the near future. These
included:

. Identification of pollutants and other ecological
hazards that are dangerous on a global scale.

. Establishment of an effective world monitoring network to keep track of these environmental dangers.

. Initiation of a global information system to facilitate exchange of experience and knowledge about environment problems.

. Establishment of internationally accepted air and water quality criteria and standards.

. Development of international guidelines for the protection of the environment.

. Achievement of comprehensive international action programs to prevent further environmental deterioration and to repair the damage already done.

. Development and improvement of training and education programs to provide the skilled capability to meet the environmental challenge.[27]

Stevenson recommended that the subcommittee maintain close coordination with the related work for the Stockholm Conference, with the appropriate specialized agencies, and with international organizations (public and private) active in the field. He suggested that the "major areas of concern might include such international machinery as may be required for determining marine pollution research priorities, for coordinating research efforts, and for collecting research information and arranging for its exchange; and regulations of deliberate disposal of materials into the ocean."[28]

Other delegates commented on the organization of work for the subcommittee and on international cooperation in scientific research.

CONCLUSION

Most forums of international diplomacy are interdependent. They follow similar patterns of action and depend more on the input of sovereign states than on innovative secretariats. And they are generally attended by the same kinds of people. Because the forums that discuss marine pollution have followed this general pattern, their resolutions and recommendations have been heavily dependent on one another and on the way in which participating states view them as vehicles for agreement.

The Stockholm Human Environment Conference departs from the general norm only in its scope. It was the first attempt to discuss environmental problems on a global scale through high-level official governmental representatives, and the first attempt of the international community to combine all single-issue environmental policy questions into one comprehensive conference. It divided its work into three levels: Level I, the intellectual-conceptual framework; Level II, the action plan level for future consideration; and Level III, actions to be completed by the conference.

Preparations for Level II and Level III activity proceeded according to the general international norm: A cautious secretariat proposing major change and then backing off in acknowledgment of national sovereignty; the preparatory committee noting the secretariat's "internationalist" recommendations and then adopting recommendations designed primarily around functional nationalistic principles; and an ever-increasing quantity of documentation and verbiage and a decreasing amount of substantive work.

The working groups formulated valuable statements of principle acknowledging the interdependence and value of the marine environment to humanity, but failed to develop innovative international solutions. States agreed to regulate what they already had the power to control, to cooperate in regions and areas in which they already had a great deal of experience, and to formulate general guidelines for pollution control, but they refused to be bound by guidelines or subject to international enforcement. And states agreed to monitor and register pollutants on a "voluntary" basis.

However, if a strong link between Level I and Level II activity develops, the Stockholm Conference could become a model for future international environmental policy-making. By developing the ingredients for a report on the state of the human environment (Level I) which identifies major areas of intellectual consensus and nonconsensus and the major gaps in present knowledge, the conference demonstrated priority issues for political leaders to consider and indicated the directions in which action should proceed (Level II). By assembling a representative group of the world's intellectual community, including leaders in the physical and social sciences, for a comprehensive reading on the present state of knowledge and opinion on the principal aspects of the relationship between man and the environment, the conference made a significant contribution.

The 1973 Law of the Sea Conference, prepared by the UN Committee on the Peaceful Uses of the Sea-Bed, was designed to develop international law for marine pollution control as part of a total regime for the continental shelf and ocean space above it. This contextual relationship obscured its importance. Informed sources believe that the formation of Subcommittee III was more political than functional. Its preparatory sessions limited discussion to general issues, confirming its low priority. Whatever agreement it may reach will not emerge as a

separate marine pollution treaty or convention. New
agreements will take the form of amendments to the 1958-
60 Geneva Conventions on the Law of the Sea.

Trends in international law and the evolution of proposals indicate that new agreements will be as vague and
general as present ones unless other major sea law issues
(military, fishing, oil exploitation) are resolved.
These trends also indicate that new agreements will involve special purpose zones adjacent to territorial waters in which coastal states will exercise "limited jurisdiction" for purposes of conservation and pollution prevention. Special purpose zones have and will continue to
be strongly resisted by states engaged in or heavily dependent upon the shipping industry. Some observers believe that IMCO--formed especially to protect and regulate such interests--is proceeding with its own conference with the intention of neutralizing or eliminating
the need for such regulatory and restrictive zones. IMCO
pollution control efforts continue to be directed toward
uniform international agreement on tanker standards, oil
releases, limited and pooled liability, and other such
arrangements that obviate the need for coastal states to
extend their jurisdictions along Canadian lines.

Due to the nature of the organization, agreement in
the IMCO forum will be limited to preventing pollution
from vessels and other carriers on the high seas. While
such regulation is important, it is ineffective without
international control over pollution releases from coasts
within national jurisdiction. Pollution release controls
on the high seas alone would not prevent the proliferation of coastal outfalls or even dumping within territorial waters. Agreement to prohibit oil discharges on the
high seas without the corresponding development of shore-
based waste reception facilities would force tanker masters to do their cleaning under the protection of dark-
ness. Historically IMCO has been largely dependent on
the willingness of the shipping industry to subject itself to international controls.

Given such limitations, IMCO agreements must be carefully scrutinized by environmentalists before treaties
reach the national ratification level. Signed conventions
are difficult to amend; the only alternative is outright
rejection with the hope of reformulation, with no interim
controls. To effectively combat marine pollution, IMCO
agreements must be tied to other arrangements beyond the
organization's own frame of reference. Regulation in
other key areas could be hastened by making national

ratification of IMCO conventions contingent upon the satisfactory negotiation of other international environmental
controls.

Finally, forums are only as significant as their participants wish them to be. The level of governmental participation in them is therefore dependent on a visibility
and public relations value. Environmental forums are most
effective when they receive worldwide press coverage and
media anticipation. Early preparations for the Stockholm
Conference were limited to technical discussions by low-
level diplomats, guided by a technical secretariat. While
these preparations were important, they lacked public relations value and failed to attract the attention they de-
served. Two years prior to the conference date, the UN
secretariat realized this deficiency and appointed an international public relations expert, Maurice Strong of
Canada, as secretary general of the conference. His leadership signaled an end to the era of "quiet" environmental
diplomacy.

NOTES

1. United Nations Conference of the Human Environment Preparatory Committee, "Draft Report," UN Doc A/
Conf.48/ PC (11)/CRP.28/Add 2, p. 4.
2. Ibid., pp. 4-5.
3. Ibid., p. 5.
4. U.N. Conference on the Human Environment Preparatory committee, "Marine Pollution: Review of Possible
Level III or Level II Actions," UN Doc A/Conf.48, p. 3.
5. Ibid., p. 4.
6. Ibid. Level III preparations include the "identification and control of pollutants and their international organizational implications."
7. Ibid., p. 5.
8. Ibid., p. 7.
9. Preparatory committee, "Draft Report," op. cit.,
p. 6.
10. Inter-Governmental Working Group on Marine Pollution (IGWGMP), "Draft Report of the First Session," UN
Doc A/Conf.48 PC/IWGMP. I/5 Prov. (London: June 18, 1971),
pp. 21-22.
11. IGWGMP, "Report of the Second Session," A/Conf.48/
IWGMP II/5 (Paris: November 22, 1971), pp. 3-5.
12. Ibid., p. 7.
13. Ibid., p. 9.

14. _Ibid._, Articles II, IV, pp. 9-10.

15. _Ibid._, Article VII, p. 10.

16. _Ibid._, Article VIII, p. 11.

17. _Ibid._, Article XI, p. 16.

18. IMCO, "UN Conference on Human Environment, Agenda Item III (a)(i): Identification and Control of Pollutants Emanating from Ships, Vessels and Other Equipment Operating in the Marine Environment," Res. 176 VI, p. 4.

19. _Ibid._, p. 5.

20. See GESAMP, "List of Noxious and Hazardous Cargoes Other than Oil," GESAMP (III/19/Annex V mimeo).

21. The International Chamber of Shipping is preparing a Tanker Safety Guide (Chemicals) in collaboration with IMCO.

22. UN Information Service, Press Release SB/17 (Geneva, February 25, 1971).

23. UN General Assembly Resolution 2750 C (XXV) of December 17, 1970. Adopted by 108 votes in favor to 7 against (Soviet Union and Warsaw Pact states), with 6 abstentions.

24. UN Press Release SB/17, _op. cit_.

25. _Ibid._ The Conference of the Committee on Disarmament concluded and opened for signature a Treaty on the Prohibition of the Emplacement of Nuclear Weapons and Other Weapons of Mass Destruction on the Seabed and the Ocean Floor and in the Subsoil Thereof on February 11, 1971.

26. UN Information Service, Press Release SB/19 (Geneva, March 12, 1971).

27. U.S. Information Service, "Statement by the Honorable J. R. Stevenson before the UN Committee on the Peaceful Uses of the Sea Bed" (March 25, 1971), pp. 2-3.

28. _Ibid._, p. 3.

6

INTELLECTUAL MODELS

   To evaluate the future of proposals for an international ocean regime and marine pollution control provisions, one must understand not only the lobbies but also
the ideas that serve as their conceptual foundations.[1]
Robert Friedheim identifies four basic models or constructs as normative inputs in the international political system: (1) normative nationalism, (2) functional
nationalism, (3) functional internationalism, and (4) normative internationalism.[2] Each proposal discussed in
Chapter 7 exhibits characteristics of each model.
   Friedheim argues that the models are useful as "heu-
ristic aids" that help to begin the analytical process,
but he also acknowledges that as analytic tools they "do
not explain anything."[3] But systems and structural-
functional analysis are useful in the context of ocean
regime,[4] especially in the analysis of specific proposals.
   The most effective models confront all ocean problems and are not limited to small optimal parts so they
acknowledge the constraints of the real world but offer
imaginative solutions to complex problems. And they are
developed through a new kind of process in which science
and politics will be intimately intertwined--a new kind
of science-politics.[5] More important from an environmental view, they must not be subordinated to "higher" or
"lower" (depending on perspective) purposes beyond the
elimination of conflict and the preservation of the marine
environment for future generations. Proposals for one
purpose that are really disguised to achieve another ought
to be identified early in debate; the problem is much too
complex and confusing to sustain ulterior motives and
wolves in sheep's clothing. Before considering and

evaluating the foremost proposals and their projected effectiveness in the control of marine pollution, the basic components of these models must be appreciated.

NORMATIVE NATIONALISM

Normative nationalists are basically oriented to ends. They argue that their respective nation-states deserve the resources of the sea to survive and prosper. They rely on the concepts of territoriality and sovereignty to justify their jurisdiction of areas beyond their geographically fixed land and internationally recognized water territories. They tend to view debate over ocean resources as a conflict situation in which resources demanded enhance one's own bargaining position while concessions to other states directly or through the international community are signs of national weakness. International control and enforcement of marine pollution is often included in the "concession" category.

Three proposals are especially characteristic of those who seek to extend the jurisdiction of their nation-states beyond present limits: (1) the expanded general purpose zone, (2) flag-state proposals, and (3) the national lakes concept.[6] Under the expanded general purpose zone, a coastal state could exclude foreign persons for most purposes and monopolize all resources for its own use (with the possible exception of innocent passage). The flag-state proposals, favored by formal and informal representatives of some nation-states advanced in ocean technology, would allow states to claim exclusive jurisdiction over sea or seabed areas and to exclude entry into the area for any unauthorized purpose. Such states would have the right to appropriate all area resources and to promulgate regulations for all those allowed access. The national lakes concept is based on fear of being excluded from an area or the right to exploit its resources.[7] Boundaries between coastal states would be set at a line every point of which is equidistant from the breadth of the territorial sea of each state. Unlike the general purpose zone concept, all water and seabed areas would be subject to national jurisdiction. As the most extreme of nationalization proposals, most experts view the national lakes concept as advantageous in the short run but fraught with long-term disadvantages.

FUNCTIONAL NATIONALISM

Functional nationalists argue that "the nation-state is still available, perhaps the most useful institution to entrust decisions requiring political and economic power."[8] Because the structure of the world system is in disorder, grand schemes of reform seem visionary, and states remain comparatively stable, they argue that the nation-state can be used deliberately to solve one segment of the overall ocean problem through the "operations analysis" process called suboptimization.[9] Their concern is to solve problems in the short run through the known practices and established administrative structure of national systems; the nation-state is viewed pragmatically as the prop or support required so a need can be fulfilled or a function carried out.[10]

Two proposals most characteristic of functional nationalism are special purpose zones and revenue lines proposals. Typical of the special purpose zones are zones for pollution control or sanitation, immigration, customs, security, hot pursuit, conservation, fishing, and mineral exploitation. Advocates of functional nationalism contend that borders are artificial creations and that certain problems, pollution among them, cannot necessarily be contained strictly within them.[11] To avoid the establishment of general purpose zones, functional nationalists believe coastal states must be allowed to extend the specific powers they deem vital to their national interests.[12]

Revenue lines proposals would assure coastal states the right to appropriate income from sea resources in proportion to the distance of the resource from the coast. The further offshore, the higher the percentage of the income that could be accredited to some international fund to assist less developed countries. Coastal states would extend domestic law and regulations beyond narrow territorial seas, offering ocean users the familiar rules available under national systems. In the extreme such an arrangement could function along the lines of the national lake concept, with the added attraction of the international sharing proposal.

FUNCTIONAL INTERNATIONALISM

Basic to all functional internationalist positions is the proposition that many problems in the interdependent world community transcend national boundaries and cannot be solved by traditional nation-state mechanisms.[13] Advocates of this approach see particular tasks that need to be done and concentrate on finding ways international agencies may do them. Some dwell solely on means while others, such as the committed political and economic functionalists, are concerned with linking means with ultimate reforms of the system as a whole.[14]

Pragmatic functionalists move into new areas because the time or circumstance may be ripe; promote or increase activities whose products are obviously useful to many; and promote activities especially susceptible to being operated by present or foreseeable intergovernmental agencies.[15] Ocean space and the control of marine pollution are viewed as fertile fields for their activities.

International registry proposals predominate the functional internationalist approach to ocean regimes. They range from the simple reciprocal validation of flag-state claims to sea areas via a recording office to elaborate international agencies to monitor and regulate exploitation and exploration. Economic functionalists support such proposals but argue further that access to common property resources must be restricted to avoid misallocation and waste. Under the present system, exploiters are in competition with no incentives to act with restraint. To eliminate the "get in and get out" mentality, functional internationalists would provide leasing powers based partially upon the market system but supplemented by administrative discretion, to provide equity for developing countries.[16]

Extensive regulatory discretion might be assigned to an international agency or conglomerate of agencies, or they could be limited to valuable but limited services. Proponents of functional internationalism both fear and hope for a reshaping of the general structure of the international system by the actions of international agencies.

NORMATIVE INTERNATIONALISM

According to Friedheim, normative internationalist proposals often share one or more of six common characteristics: (1) concern for the central problems of world politics; (2) awareness that the end sought is the development of a sense of world community; (3) concentration on problems of conflict; (4) concern for formal organization, particularly insistence upon development of international enforcement mechanisms; (5) sense of an ethical obligation to redistribute the world's wealth; and (6) an attempt to provide the United Nations with a source of independent income.[17] Their solutions for ocean problems tend to be part of a grand design for the larger problems of the world,[18] and their proposals tend to shift the sovereign powers of nation-states to an international organization representing all the people of the world. They are characterized by deductive thinking in which general laws are discerned from general trends and learned axioms applied to specific situations.

Normative internationalists generally believe that, without world political community, chaos is inevitable; preventing the cataclysm is the priority effort. They see the oceans as potential areas in which the international community can control conflict, alter the allocation of resources, and perhaps develop a model of international cooperation for terrestrial application. They sense the danger that the political problems of man on land will be transferred to the sea unless new systems of governance are developed.

Opponents to such schemes argue that grand designs possess too many technical imperfections,[19] and that their "all or nothing" characteristic renders many non-negotiable and inflexible. Others indicate their concern that "international organization is presently too weak as a governmental or administrative mechanism to manage the sea directly."[20] Some governments argue that such proposals are attacks upon the basis of their particular existence,[21] while others contend that the principal posts of command in such systems would inevitably "be in the hands of the capitalist monopolies of certain imperialist powers."[22]

NOTES

1. For support of this concept, see Edward Miles, "Organizations and Integration in International Systems," International Studies Quarterly 12, no. 2 (June 1968).

2. See Robert L. Friedheim, Understanding the Debate on Ocean Resources (Denver: University of Denver, 1969).

3. Ibid., p. 2.

4. For criticism of the method, see A. James Gregor, "Political Science and the Use of Functional Analysis," The American Political Science Review 62, no. 2 (June 1968): 425-39; Martin Landau, "On the Use of Functional Analysis in American Political Science," Social Research 35, no. 1 (Spring 1968): 48-75.

5. Clifton Fadiman and Jean White, eds., _Ecocide and Thoughts Toward Survival_ (New York: Interbook, 1971), p. 9.

6. Friedheim, _op. cit._, p. 5.

7. See Seymour Bernfeld, "Developing the Resources of the Sea--Security of Investment," _The International Lawyer_ 2 (1967): 67.

8. Friedheim, _op. cit._, p. 9.

9. See Roland McKean, _Efficiency in Government Through Systems Analysis: With Emphasis on Water Resources Development_ (New York: Wiley, 1958), p. 29; Charles J. Hitch, "Suboptimization in Operations Problems," _Journal of the Operations Research Society of America_, May 1953, pp. 87-94.

10. Friedheim, _op. cit._, p. 9.

11. See Douglas M. Johnston, "New Uses of International Law in the North Pacific," _Washington Law Review_ 43, no. 1 (October 1967): 85, for characterization of functional regimes as the "wave of the future."

12. See Louis Henkin, _Law for the Sea's Mineral Resources_, ISHA Monograph No. 1 (New York: Columbia University Press, 1968), p. 24.

13. See Karl W. Deutch _et al._, _Political Community and the North Atlantic Area_ (Princeton, N.J.: Princeton University Press, 1957) for an attack on this notion.

14. See writings of David Mitrany, James P. Sewell, and Ernst B. Haas for fundamentals of functional internationalism.

15. Friedheim, _op. cit._, p. 15.

16. See Francis T. Christy, _New Dimensions for the United Nations_ (Dobbs Ferry, N.Y.: Oceana, 1966); "Panel: Conflict of Uses of the Sea," in L. M. Alexander, ed., _The Law of the Sea: The Future of the Sea's Resources_ (Kingston: University of Rhode Island, 1970).

17. Friedheim, _op. cit._, p. 30.

18. See Sylvester Hemleben, _Peace Plans Through Six Centuries_ (Chicago: University of Chicago Press, 1943) for grand design approaches predating the modern nation-state.

19. William T. Burke, "A Negative View of a Proposal for United Nations Ownership of Ocean Mineral Resources," _National Resource Lawyer_ 1, no. 2 (June 1968): 42-62.

20. Daniel S. Cheever, "The Role of International Organization in Ocean Development," _International Organization_ 22, no. 3 (1968): 648.

21. See the views of some Latin American States in untitled UN Doc mimeo, A/C.1/PV.1526, pp. 23-25; A/C.1/PV.1527, pp. 8-32.

22. Untitled UN Doc mimeo, A/C.1/PV.1592, p. 17 (Soviet Union).

7

THE PROPOSALS

Each of the following ocean regime proposals rests on one of the conceptual models discussed in Chapter 6. Most are specifically designed to encourage exploration and exploitation of ocean resources and to distribute derivative revenues. Each addresses ecological and pollution control considerations, but security and economic considerations are dominant. This emphasis is directly related to the lack of international environmental interest groups.

This chapter describes and critiques the major ocean regime proposals of the last decade, focusing primarily on their provisions for marine pollution control. Proposals emanating from official conferences and governments are given greater weight since they are closer to actual enactment than those of private groups and individuals. Private proposals provide idealized approaches to pollution problems that are uncompromised by national interest groups. They provide insight and imagination otherwise not available at the international level.

This analysis emphasizes pragmatic solutions to marine pollution problems. The available scientific evidence justifies enacting programs and agreements at the earliest possible date; procrastination merely limits alternatives.

Serious proposals for the international control of marine resources began to emerge at the close of World War II. In 1950 the International Law Commission (ILC), a legal arm of the United Nations, rejected a motion to entrust continental shelf exploitation to the international community because of "insurmountable difficulties."[1] The concept emerged repeatedly in subsequent ILC discussions and was resolved (temporarily) by the adoption of the 1958 Continental Shelf Convention. Under this treaty coastal nations have the right to establish rules and regulations for continental shelf exploitation beyond the limits of their national jurisdiction according to the indefinite "exploitability criterion." They have the right to enforce oil pollution regulations and, with the exception of those dependent upon the International Atomic Energy Agency (IAEA) for fissionable materials, to regulate the sea disposal of radioactive wastes.

In 1957 the Commission to Study the Organization of Peace recommended that the United Nations establish an organization to claim jurisdiction and control over the seabed beneath the high seas, with recommendatory powers over fishing on the high seas and binding powers to prevent pollution of the marine environment.[2] The commission believed its plan could be enacted without charter revision. In a model revision of the United Nations charter, however, Grenville Clark and Louis Sohn provided under a revised article that the United Nations would itself exercise a trusteeship over the high seas and certain rivers.[3] A 1965 White House Conference on International Cooperation[4] and 1965 report of the Commission to Study the Organization of Peace[5] both recommended that the United Nations undertake responsibility for leasing and controlling the exploitation of the seabed.

While many prominent government officials endorsed this concept, specific proposals were limited to nongovernment sources. Ambassador Arvid Pardo of Malta introduced the first comprehensive national revision of sea law to the United Nations General Assembly in August 1967. Pardo proposed an extensive new treaty to prevent national appropriation of unclaimed seabeds, to reserve those areas exclusively for peaceful uses, to restrict the definition of the continental shelf, and to provide distribution machinery to allocate "common heritage" resource income to developing countries through the United Nations.[6] Pardo estimated that internationalized seabed income and extraction royalties would net $5 billion for the UN treasury by 1975.

The Pardo proposal prompted the General Assembly to establish a Committee on the Peaceful Uses of the Sea-Bed to consider

> a broad range of related issues, including
> those concerning the regimes of the high
> sea, the continental shelf, the territorial

sea (including the question of its breadth
and the question of international straits)
and contiguous zone, fishing and conservation of the living resources of the high
seas (including the question of the preferential rights of the coastal State),
the preservation of the marine environment
(including, inter alia, the preservation
of the marine environment from pollution)
and scientific research, and to arrive in
1973, if possible, a conference on the law
of the sea which would establish an equitable regime.[7]

It also stimulated high-level debate and a flood of proposals for governing and regulating the use of the sea.[8]

PRINCIPLES PROPOSED BY SENATOR CLAIBORNE PELL

One of the first detailed model treaties on the
structure of an ocean regime was presented by U.S. Senator Claiborne Pell in Senate Resolutions 172 and 186 of
the last session of the ninetieth U.S. Congress. Although
it carried no official government approval, the Pell draft
incorporated Ambassador Pardo's basic thesis of utilizing
international ocean resources for the benefit and interests of all mankind. To insure peaceful and orderly exploitation of the natural resources of the seabed, Pell
proposed that states party to the treaty "undertake to
engage in such authority to be designed by the United Nations and to be independent of any State."[9] Licenses
would be issued "consistent with the conservation of and
prevention of the waste of natural resources of the seabed and subsoil of ocean space . . . to provide for the
most efficient exploitation of resources possible."[10] A
state or international organization holding a license
would be obliged to undertake, in the area covered by
such license, all appropriate measures for the protection
of the living resources of the sea from harmful agents
and would pursue its activities so as to avoid the harmful contamination of the environment.[11] No installations
or devices could be established where interference would
be caused to the use of recognized sea lanes essential to
international commerce and navigation.[12]
Disputes over compliance with license provisions
would be handled by the licensing authority; in the event

that the authority did not render a decision within a
reasonable period of time, such disputes would, at the
request of any of the parties, be submitted to a standing
review panel appointed by the International Court of Justice.[13] Coastal states would regulate exploitation of
the continental shelf to a depth of 550 meters or a distance of 50 miles, whichever was greater.[14] The disposal
of radioactive waste material in ocean space would be subject to safety regulations prescribed by IAEA in consultation with the licensing authority.[15]

The most interesting concept in the Pell proposal--
and the one that most others lack--is the establishment
of a permanent force, the Sea Guard of the United Nations,
to take action necessary to maintain and enforce international compliance with the provisions of the treaty.[16]
The Sea Guard would be under the control of the Security
Council of the United Nations and the licensing authority.

Critique

The Pell draft treaty is modeled after the Treaty of
Outer Space and specifically designed to steer a middle
course between the Maltese (Pardo) and flag-state approaches. It was intended to accommodate the "various
political, military, economic, and scientific aspects of
this issue, recognizing that there are as many valid interests as there are individual states."[17] The Pell proposal accomplished these limited objectives through a
functional licensing approach, but lacked the detail vital
to any international agreement on ocean space. It vested
regulatory functions in an international authority but
failed to define the extent of that authority. It placed
control of the Sea Guard with the UN Security Council but
failed to provide protection against the national veto
that has so effectively impaired UN peacekeeping functions. It gave responsibility for enforcing vague pollution control measures to an international authority but
failed to fully confront the "flags of convenience" dodge.

The evolution of functions and organs of any body
are mutually dependent. Diplomats hesitate to spell out
precise functions without knowing the nature of the organs
that will exercise them, for fear that the functions may
be exercised very badly, distorted past recognition, or
never performed at all.[18]

The main virtue of the Pell draft treaty is that it
explores to the limit the applicability of outer space law

to ocean space. It accords international nongovernmental
organizations a status almost equal to that of nations.
And it is very specific in the powers it gives to the
licensing agency.[19]

THE DANZIG TREATY

In 1968 the UN World Peace Through Law Center advanced Pell's concepts in a new draft treaty. Known as
the Danzig draft (after the center's chairman, Aaron
Danzig), it recognized that "the interdependence of the
ocean bed and the ocean waters is an inescapable fact
with ineluctable legal consequences."[20] It recommended
that an Ocean Agency be structured along the lines of the
United Nations Special Fund, in which votes are evenly
divided between technologically advanced nations and developing countries, with a two-thirds majority required
for action. The agency would have the power to grant licenses and other forms of authority to both states and
nongovernment entitles to exploit the seabed. Its function would be primarily economic in license allocation,
as well as fostering and protecting scientific research
and development. The Danzig draft proposed that the agency's governing body be elected by the UN Economic and Social Council. Income derived from license allocation beyond that used to defray costs would be paid to the United
Nations.

The Danzig draft treaty further elaborated on Pell's
proposal by creating a special Ocean Tribunal before
which states, nongovernmental organizations, and persons
would have standing.[21] Appeals from the tribunal's determinations could be taken by means of an Ocean Agency
request for an advisory opinion. As a condition of such
appeal, litigants would stipulate in advance that they
would be bound by such advisory opinion.

Critique

The emphasis of the Danzig draft was primarily economic, designed to promote exploitation and to distribute
license revenues to the United Nations. No provision was
made for environmental appeals. No detailed descriptions
of conditions under which the Ocean Agency might deny or
withdraw a license were included.

The Ocean Tribunal was the most significant concept contributed to further treaty development. Major weaknesses emerged in the difficult problem of collaboration between free enterprise and socialist nations.

THE BORGESE DRAFT

The Center for the Study of Democratic Institutions organized three conferences between February and June of 1968 to learn the opinions of international ocean experts. These gatherings produced a draft statute by the chairman, Elizabeth Mann Borgese, and two ambitious conferences entitled Pacem in Maribus 1 and 2 on the island of Malta in the summers of 1970 and 1971.[22] These conferences used the Borgese draft as a point of departure for comprehensive sea law considerations; therefore, much comment and criticism on its positive and negative characteristics is available. However, little has been said about the quality of its method for controlling marine pollution.

The Borgese international ocean regime would regulate "all activities on the high seas and on or under the seabed."[23] One of thirteen defined functions would authorize the regime to "issue regulations concerning pollution and the disposal of radioactive waste material in ocean space."[24] Ocean space is defined as "the high seas, the territorial seas, the territorial waters, and contiguous zones, the atmosphere above it, the continental shelf, the seabed and what is below it."[25]

The international ocean regime would function through four basic institutions: a Maritime Commission, a Maritime Assembly, a Maritime Planning Agency, and a Maritime Court. Subordinate to these institutions would be maritime secretariats for ocean mining, deep sea oil extraction, fisheries and aquaculture, and others as necessary, and regional arrangements to meet special needs.

The Maritime Assembly would consist of four chambers of 81 delegates each. The first chamber, elected by the UN General Assembly, would represent all the regions of the world. The second, elected in a manner to be determined, would represent international mining corporations, organizations, unions, producers, and consumers directly interested in the extraction of oil, metals, minerals, and other nonliving resources from the seabed. The third would represent fishing organizations, processors, merchants, and other fishery-oriented interests. The fourth would represent scientists interested in ocean affairs.[26]

A majority vote of the political chamber and another chamber competent in the matter voted upon would prevail. The major duties of the Maritime Assembly would be to determine rules and regulations for issuing licenses and for the conservation and exploitation of the ocean's living resources. The Maritime Assembly would also elect the Maritime Commission's members and approve their actions.

The Maritime Commission would have seventeen members, five representing the most advanced nations in ocean-space technology and twelve elected with due regard to equitable representation of developed and developing nations, maritime and landlocked states, and nations operating under free enterprise and socialistic economic systems.[27] Decisions on the regime's development plans and budgets would require a two-thirds majority of those present and voting. Decisions on other questions would be made by majority vote. The Maritime Commission would have the authority to carry out the regime's functions in accord with the treaty, subject to its responsibilities to the Maritime Assembly. Decisions concerning pollution and security would be self-executing, without need of approval by the Maritime Assembly.[28]

The Marine Planning Agency (composed of expert economists, scientists, and administrators) would be responsible for coordinating all international organizational projects and efforts. It would prepare plans to "maximize development and exploitation of living and non-living resources and to ensure their conservation."[29] It would prepare the regime's budget, redistribute fee revenues, and protect developing countries from price fluctuations on minerals and metals extracted from the oceans.

The Maritime Court, composed of eleven judges by agreement of the governments of member states, would have jurisdiction over appeals for annulment of decisions and recommendations of the regime on the grounds of lack of legal competence, substantial procedural violations, violation of the statute or of any rule of law relating to its application, or a use of power.[30]

Critique

The Borgese draft is based on the premise that the oceans constitute a unified global system whose problems cannot be resolved through unilateral action. It concludes that a supranational authority is needed to regulate ocean usage and resources in the long-term interests of all mankind. It essentially denies that coastal states have special or inherent rights in adjacent oceans and seabeds. It proposes that an ocean regime be designed to maintain peace and order, to enforce safety rules and antipollution regulations, to conserve exhaustible resources, to conduct scientific research, to issue exploitation licenses, to collect royalties, and to adjudicate maritime disputes. As such the Borgese model represents the most normative and comprehensive internationalist proposal for governing the uses of the sea.

In its recognition of the interdependence of the seabed and the superadjacent waters, the Borgese plan is environmentally useful. Drilling and spilling, detonations and installations on and below the seabed, are bound to affect the waters above. Marine pollution, like metropolitan sprawl, disrupts vegetal and animal ecology, making a myth of the freedom of the seas.[31] Logically, Mrs. Borgese argues, planning the industrialization of the seabed must be accompanied by planning of antipollution measures and the conservation of marine life. Industry, fishery, communications, and the military complex are all linked. Jurisdiction over one ocean activity involves jurisdiction over others. To "regulate" ocean exploitation, a regime must acknowledge and provide for the vertical interdependence of ocean space and for the functional interdependence of ocean activities. Pollution and fish recognize no political boundaries, nor can they be regulated without harmonization of controls in all ocean jurisdictional subdivisions (Mrs. Borgese terms this "horizontal interdependence"). She concludes, "If it is to be effective, the Regime must deal, therefore, with ocean space as an indivisible ecological whole."[32]

Mrs. Borgese does not believe that the establishment of a world government for the oceans would necessarily mean the invasion of national sovereignty. She anticipates that planning would transform and enlarge the concept of law and strengthen the regime's jurisdiction in two dimensions: on a functional scale, according to subject matter, and on a geographic scale, whether vertical or horizontal. On a functional scale, the regime could issue anything from binding regulations on matters of security and pollution to recommendations on matters of fishing or communications. On a territorial scale, it could issue binding regulations concerning the seabed, recommendations concerning the high seas or superadjacent waters, and opinions concerning territorial waters and submarine areas under national jurisdiction.[33]

The precise language of the draft treaty, however, suggests quite the opposite. No provision is made for the "scaled" use of international power. Rather, the international ocean regime would function as a world government empowered to control ocean space from its depths to its beaches; the intent to establish world government is clear. According to Mrs. Borgese, "the seabed was the lever, the ocean is the bridge. The goal is world order."[34] The proposed ocean regime is tailored to achieve that goal.

Despite its attractiveness as a pollution control convention, the Borgese draft can serve only as an ideal model from which to glean possible applications for treaty formulation in the "real world." It fails to accommodate the power realities and interests that now determine sea law. Its orientation provides a conception of how things could be if the sea, like outer space, were a vacuum. More important, it demonstrates a way by which the international community might make the transition from representational democracy to participational democracy in a rational approach to the world's most critical future problem.

THE UNITED KINGDOM WORKING PAPER

Following the introduction by the United States of a draft Convention on the International Seabed Area on August 3, 1970, certain states of Western Europe presented their own working papers to the Committee on the Peaceful Uses of the Sea-Bed. The similarities between them, particularly the French and British proposals, were not entirely coincidental, offering evidence of the progress toward European economic integration.

Consensus among Western European states was primarily due to a working agreement on the division of the North Sea's continental shelf for oil and mineral exploitation. After extensive negotiation and international arbitration, North Sea border states divided the North Sea shelf into "blocks" or lots for lease to private companies by the states. National jurisdiction over the blocks was determined by extending territorial borders out to equidistant median lines in the North Sea.

The British, French, and other European seabed proposals reflected this North Sea experience by maintaining an approach with national jurisdiction over international resources. They recommended that an international body be established only to "equitably" allocate seabed exploitation licenses among nation-states in areas outside national jurisdiction. In the 1970 British working paper the agreement, like its North Sea model, would:

> provide for division of the whole of the
> seabed outside national jurisdiction into
> areas (called "blocks" and possibly defined by reference to coordinates of latitude and longitude) large enough to permit
> of efficient exploration and exploitation,
> but small enough to allow fair opportunities to all States parties to the agreement.
> Different kinds of resources [would] require
> different sizes of blocks. These sizes
> [would] be influenced by geological and economic factors (including the depth of water
> at the site of operations, distance from
> land and from sources of supplies, and
> kinds of equipment necessary).[35]

These blocks would be allocated proportionately to each signatory state on a first come-first served basis or, failing agreement in the event of a conflict, "by determination of the international body based solely on random selection by computer."[36]

The regime proposed by the British working paper would be composed of a Board of Governors elected by a plenary conference of states party to the treaty.[37] Board powers would be limited to governing seabed exploration and issuing exploitation licenses. The agreement would specifically provide that "the establishment of the regime . . . not affect the legal status of the superadjacent waters as high seas or that of the air space above those waters."[38]

The British working paper further recommended that a regime provide for:

1. The prevention and control of pollution of the marine environment resulting from research into and exploration of the area, or exploitation of its natural resources.
2. The conservation of the natural resources of the area.[39]

Each state would be responsible to the international body for ensuring that its sublicensees, whether working in blocks or under a nonexclusive license, follow operating rules determined by the agreement. The operating rules would include waste prevention in resource development and the prevention of pollution damage to other resources or the environment.[40] The international body could, under clearly defined arrangements, inspect operations to ensure that required standards were being observed. Provisions governing liability for damage to living sea resources and state coasts would also be included.

Critique

Many critics charge that the North Sea or "checkerboard squares" model of block licensing does not provide adequate environmental protection controls. It is unclear precisely who will do what enforcing and where.[41] Although this critique can be applied to most other special purpose zone proposals, it is more crucial under the terms of the British working paper. The British proposal does not establish specific regulatory authority and responsibility within each square, nor does it clearly outline the method of making regulations compatible. It does not stipulate that the squares be the same size for different commodities, but makes no provisions for multiplicity of use. And the British proposal, like others, proceeds from the assumed right to exploit, which subordinates marine pollution control.

The North Sea model of cooperation, however, has value for future regional pollution control arrangements. Substantial agreement in the jurisdiction area permitted a major regional marine pollution convention for the Northeast Atlantic: the Convention for the Prevention of Marine Pollution by Dumping from Ships and Aircraft, signed at Oslo in February 1972.[42] Contracting parties agreed to prohibit or regulate dumping in parts of the Atlantic and Arctic Oceans[43] and to adopt measures to prevent the diversion of dumping of harmful substances into areas outside the convention's jurisdiction.[44] Except in cases of force majeure or where the substances occur only as trace contaminants in waste to which they have not been added for the purpose of being dumped,[45] contracting parties agreed to prohibit the sea disposal of organohalogen compounds, organosilicon compounds, mercury and mercury compounds, cadmium and cadmium compounds, plastics and other persistents, and substances likely to be carcinogenic under the conditions of disposal.[46]

Other pollutants, such as lead, arsenic, copper, zinc, cyanides, and fluorides, pesticides and their by-products, and substances that might reduce amenities or present serious obstacles to fishing or navigation, would have to be dumped under specific permits in areas not less than 150 nautical miles from the nearest land and in depths not less than 2,000 meters.[47]

While nothing in the convention abridges the sovereign immunity to which certain vessels are entitled under international law, and while enforcement of the convention is left solely to the individual contracting parties on national levels, the agreement indicates progressive developments in international environmental law. The convention established a supervisory commission of regional representatives to review dumping permits and related records, to review the efficacy of the control measures adopted, and to recommend amendments, additions, or deletions.[48] As such, it represents one of the most effective regional pollution control arrangements yet devised.

The North Sea model of jurisdiction may present problems of global application, but it does seem to work on a regional basis. Once the shelf was divided, agreement on pollution control followed. This may be due more to the high economic integration of the region or to the fact that the North and Baltic Seas are easily recognized as two of the world's worst polluted. Nevertheless, its apparent functional success should not be discounted for future regional application.

THE U.S. DRAFT SEABED TREATY

In August 1970 the U.S. government introduced a draft convention on the seabed in the United Nations Committee on the Peaceful Uses of the Sea-Bed.[49] The draft, in conjunction with supplemental working papers, represented the basic negotiating position for U.S. diplomats in the 1973-74 Law of the Sea Conference. Most comment and discussion of the draft relates to its potential international acceptability and its functional nationalistic approach to world affairs.[50] Only limited discussion has been directed to its marine pollution control provisions.

The U.S. draft did not incorporate all the recommendations of the U.S. Commission on Marine Science, Engineering and Resources, although its authors relied heavily on the commission's 1969 panel reports in formulating each

draft article.[51] The commission did not have "sufficient
opportunity to study the problems of oceanic pollution"
and could "make no recommendations in this area."[52] Its
international panel evaluated the existing framework within which marine pollution problems were being handled and
found it "deficient in important respects."[53] The inter-
departmental committee that wrote the U.S. draft did not
have the benefit of an extensive pollution prevention
study prior to their work.

    The primary concern of the drafting group was to in-
tegrate the positions and interests of the Defense, Interior, Transportation, and other departments and agencies and produce a negotiable document of potential international acceptability. This emphasis also was adopted by
the Interagency Task Force on Law of the Sea in its efforts to "accommodate the total national interest rather
than any particular segment of it."[54] The purpose of this
discussion is to examine the marine pollution control provisions of this draft and subsequent working papers to determine whether there is an inherent or inevitable conflict
between accommodating the total national interest and promoting effective international regulation of ocean pollution.

    The U.S. draft proposes that the seabed be divided
into three zones: the territorial seabed, the international trusteeship area, and the international seabed
area. A simultaneously proposed convention on the width
of the territorial sea would fix the boundary of exclusive
national jurisdiction to a maximum of twelve, as opposed
to three, miles from coasts over all sea-seabed activities.
National jurisdiction on seabed activities alone would extend to the 200-meter isobath adjacent to the coasts of
continents and islands.[55] There would be no exclusive
jurisdiction over activities in the water column above
outside the proposed twelve-mile limit. Coastal states
would promulgate rules and regulations for the exploration
and exploitation of seabed resources and for the control
of marine pollution in this zone.

    The international seabed area would include the en-
tire ocean bottom and substrata seaward of the 200-meter
isobath. For revenue purposes a trusteeship area would
be established between the twelve-mile limit and a line
where the downward inclination of the seabed surface
reached an "unspecified" gradient. U.S. State Department
officials have informally indicated their desire to have
this area extend to the base of the continental rise. A
portion of licensing and royalty revenues collected by

coastal states in this area would be returned to the international community. Beyond the trusteeship area, states would bid for exploitation rights in blocks of 500 square kilometers for oil, 40,000 square kilometers for other minerals. Coastal states would enforce marine pollution control regulations "in trust" for the international community and abide by whatever standards it established.

Rules and recommended practices containing these standards would be adopted by an international commission and placed in the annexes of the proposed convention.[56] The draft requires that they be developed to "assure that all exploration and exploitation activities, and all deep drilling, are conducted with strict and adequate safeguards for the protection of human life and the marine environment."[57]

The U.S. draft delegates responsibility for environmental damage to contracting parties (states) that sponsor or authorize activities in the international area.[58] The draft authorizes the establishment of an International Seabed Resource Authority to ensure the protection of the marine environment against pollution from "drilling, dredging, excavation, waste disposal, and the construction, operation, or maintenance of installations, pipelines, and other devices."[59] The authority would have supervisory powers over seabed areas that coastal states delegated to it, and inspection duties throughout the international trusteeship area.

The authority would be composed of three principal organs: an assembly, a council, and a tribunal. The assembly would represent all contracting states and would have general authority to approve budgets, to amend the convention, and to approve actions of and elect members to the council. The U.S. draft requires that council members be elected to include the six most industrially advanced contracting parties and eighteen other contracting parties of which at least twelve would be developing countries of equitable geographic distribution.

The council would be empowered to issue emergency orders at the request of any contracting party to prevent serious harm to the marine environment.[60] These orders would be communicated immediately to licensees and their authorizing or sponsoring governments. The council could also provide emergency relief and assistance funds in the event of a marine environment disaster caused by exploration or exploitation.

The tribunal would decide all disputes relating to the interpretation and application of the draft convention.

It would be empowered to levy fines of $1,000 per day and award damages to aggrieved parties if it should determine that a contracting party or licensee failed to fulfill any of its obligations as described in the draft convention. Unless directed by a trustee or sponsoring party, gross and persistent violations of the convention's provisions would be grounds for revoking licenses. Council emergency orders and license revocations would be reviewed by the tribunal when so requested by a contracting party, and could be suspended if found unwarranted.[61]

Licensees and their sponsoring states would be liable for damage to other users of the marine environment. While the limits of that liability are not defined, the draft convention would require operators to guarantee financial responsibility by subscribing to some form of insurance plan.

States party to the convention would be permitted to impose operating safety, conservation, and pollution standards for seabed activities higher than those established by the Seabed Resource Authority.[62] They would also have the option of imposing additional sanctions when applicable standards were violated in areas under their jurisdiction.

Critique

The United States has sought to bring ocean pollution under effective international regulation consistent with its domestic interests in a variety of forums. It has enjoyed successful international cooperation through the Intergovernmental Maritime Consultative Organization, the Stockholm Conference on the Human Environment, and the London Conference on Ocean Dumping. The United States believes that further work is urgently needed to ensure effective protection of the oceans. However, it does not believe "that the Seabed Committee [has] the expertise to deal adequately with the technical aspects of these complex problems" or that the specific problems involved in controls on land-based sources of pollution are appropriate for negotiation at the Law of the Sea Conference.[63] It has argued that these problems must be handled primarily by national and local governments and through regional cooperation.[64]

The U.S. State Department has therefore taken the position that the Seabed Committee and the Law of the Sea Conference should develop draft treaty articles "stating

the _general_ principles governing the common effort to ensure that man's use of the oceans and their resources is
carried out in harmony with the environment and with a
minimum of risk of pollution."[65] It has recommended that
Marine Pollution Subcommittee III concentrate its attention on certain aspects of pollution from vessels and on
basic legal principles dealing with marine pollution.
These principles, drawn from the conclusions of the Stockholm Conference, could in turn form the "basis for draft
treaty articles of a _general_ nature."[66] In less diplo-
matic terms, the United States sees little purpose in Subcommittee III other than general discussion.

However, the United States does consider the question of pollution from exploration and exploitation of
the seabed appropriate for the Seabed Committee and the
Law of the Sea Conference to resolve. The U.S. draft seabed treaty proposes that an international seabed organization be established by the conference, with broad regulatory and emergency powers to prevent pollution. And the
draft provides intermediate zones on the seabeds so that

> minimum environmental standards can be
> fixed internationally, thus better assur-
> ing protection of the ocean environment
> as a whole, assuring coastal states that
> they will not suffer competitive economic
> disadvantage by applying such standards,
> and assuring coastal states not only the
> right to apply higher standards if they
> choose but the right to seek technical
> assistance from the international author-
> ity in doing so.[67]

In the view of the United States, the right of a
coastal state to apply marine pollution control standards
for seabed exploitation in its trusteeship area that are
higher than minimum internationally accepted criteria
does not translate or apply to coastal state control of
pollution from vessels beyond the twelve-mile territorial
sea. Fearful that "international interests in freedom of
navigation could be seriously compromised by coastal
state controls over vessels and their movement,"[68] the
United States contends that only a system of exclusively
international standards will do.

The logic of this double standard is politically
clear but environmentally unjustifiable. It also contra-
dicts the recommendations of the secretary of state's

advisory committee on the Stockholm Conference.[69] By extending national jurisdiction (not sovereignty) over
large seabed areas, the desire of the oil industry to
work within a secure framework and to negotiate individual royalty payments is met. By insisting that coastal
states cannot supplement and enforce international pollution standards on the high seas beyond twelve miles, the
national security interest in unhampered navigation and
the desire of the transportation industry to avoid increased shipping costs is satisfied. But exclusively international standards do not meet the special needs of
the ocean's highly variegated geographic regions and climates. Physical variations in the nature of the areas
and the resources involved make universal rules and regulations difficult. According to most ocean experts, "The
belief that the world ocean is a relatively homogeneous
physical body for which simple rules and regulations can
be developed" is a myth.[70]

A political compromise of the total national interest in draft treaty formulation had two additional environmental disadvantages. By limiting standing before
the tribunal to contracting parties, the draft needlessly
limits the right of third parties to redress of grievance.
Private persons and groups would bear the burden of proof
in persuading their own or other governments to "press
charges" against one another. The realities of international politics dictate that such action would take place
only, if ever, in extreme and obviously hazardous situations.[71] The cumulative effects of all the situations
that did not meet this criterion could be disastrous for
the marine environment. Designed to facilitate offshore
resource exploitation, the draft has few of the "functional brakes necessary to slow or prohibit development"
even if coastal states desire to enhance other uses and
protect coastal zones.[72] The lure of lucrative oil exploitation royalties and industrialization is difficult
for the most environmentally conscious developing country.
There are few incentives to be clean.

In summary the U.S. position on the law of the sea
is politically defensible and economically understandable
but in many respects environmentally weak. These defects
are not insurmountable. The U.S. draft treaty exhibits
several potentially desirable and innovative marine pollution control features, despite its functional nationalistic approach to sea law. The council's power to issue
emergency orders to prevent serious marine pollution and
the tribunal's authority to levy fines, award damages,

and revoke licenses represent important evolutions toward effective international control of marine pollution. Without a flexible definition of an "emergency" or provisions minimizing the influence of economic considerations on council members, the environmental effectiveness of these innovations could be compromised. Ecological imperatives require expert scientific judgment, not political expediency. By broadening access to injunctive relief, the draft could eliminate the unnecessary burden of persuading "middlemen" contracting states to seek action. "The major defect in many regulations aimed at controlling pollution has been that they reach either too small a part of the spectrum of polluters or that they reach the wrong party."[73]

More important, the entire U.S. position must adopt the flexibility of the seabed draft and provide for the special needs and physical differences of regions that require more stringent pollution control standards than the lowest common denominator international compromise can produce. It is not ecologically justifiable to advocate the right of coastal states to apply higher standards on the seabed while not recognizing special situations and equal rights to protect the waters above. Scientific experts should make recommendations for basic minimum requirements and for the special needs of certain regions. As Lewis M. Alexander has said, "We must be prepared to respond effectively to unilateral actions by other governments concerning jurisdiction over these physical anomalies; a corollary to this is that our response need not always be negative."[74]

THE MALTESE DRAFT OCEAN SPACE TREATY

In August 1971 Arvid Pardo presented Malta's Draft Ocean Space Treaty to the UN Committee on the Peaceful Uses of the Sea-Bed.[75] In an extensive document of 205 articles, Malta's permanent ambassador for ocean affairs proposed the abolition of the continental shelf convention and a revolution in political theory.[76] While the draft treaty established "national" and "international" zones, it postulated one ocean space in the belief that the old continental shelf theory and the national needs it served were obsolete.

The first 80 articles cover the whole range of ocean activities in national and international ocean space, including the control of pollution, in great detail. Comment and criticism on many of the proposed regulations is available;[77] however, analysis of the approach to marine pollution control is scanty.

Part I, Chapter II, Article 2, formulates two principles Pardo believed should be incorporated into international law:

> Firstly, that no State can legitimately use its technological capability, whether within or outside national jurisdiction, in a manner that may cause extensive change in the naturalast of the marine environment, without consent of the international community;
>
> Secondly, that the coastal State has a legal obligation to take and enforce within its jurisdiction reasonable measures to control pollution of the oceans which might cause substantial injury to the interests of other States.[78]

To provide a framework for these principles, Pardo proposed that national jurisdiction (not sovereignty) be extended to belts of ocean space 200 nautical miles wide around continents and islands. Ocean areas beyond 200 nautical miles would constitute international ocean space, no part of which would be subject to any kind of national jurisdiction unless expressly provided in the convention.[79] Coastal states would not be able to hamper vessel passage through national ocean space except within a belt of sea not exceeding twelve nautical miles in breadth adjacent to their coasts. Within this twelve-mile limit a coastal state could: (1) prevent passage that was not innocent; (2) suspend temporarily in specified areas the innocent passage of foreign vessels if such suspension was essential for the protection of its security; (3) take the steps necessary to prevent any breach of the conditions to which admission of vessels to international waters is subject.[80] Foreign vessels crossing national ocean space would be required to comply with the rules and regulations relating to transport, navigation, and the prevention of pollution.[81] In national ocean space a coastal state could reserve to its nationals the exploitation of natural resources,[82] but it would be required to consult with other states and international ocean space institutions before undertaking or permitting activities that might substantially reduce the living resources of ocean space outside its jurisdiction.[83] Coastal states would be able to license or engage in other uses of national ocean space provided that

> Special precautions are taken in the con-
> struction and siting of installations con-
> taining radio-active materials, petroleum
> or other substances which may cause dele-
> terious effects to the living resources or
> to the quality of the marine environment.
> No such installations [can] be constructed
> in areas subject to frequent earthquakes or
> in areas where interference may be caused
> to the use of recognized sealanes essential
> to international navigation.[84]

International ocean space (IOS) would be administered by four IOS Institutions: an assembly, a council, an international maritime court, and a secretariat,[85] in the name and on behalf of the international community.[86] The concept of common heritage, previously applied only to the seabed, would be extended to ocean space.[87] "All activities in International Ocean Space [would] be conducted with strict and adequate safeguards for the protection of human life and for the protection of the marine environment."[88] Exploration and exploitation of natural resources would not be permitted in areas of international ocean space where scientific findings indicated the probability that exploitation might result in extensive pollution of the marine environment.[89] Each contracting party would bear international responsibility for national activities or for activities under its sponsorship in international ocean space, whether such activities were performed by governmental agencies, nongovernmental agencies, or individuals.[90]

The IOS institutions would regulate and control the disposal of radioactive wastes in IOS in consultation with the IAEA. In cooperation with IAEA, they also would maintain a register of radioactive releases in IOS. Nuclear and thermonuclear explosions of whatever nature would be prohibited in IOS.[91]

The IOS institutions could also regulate the introduction of substances, whether solid or liquid or gaseous, or of energy into IOS or the airspace above, whether for disposal or for other purposes, if in quantities that might reasonably be expected to produce significant deleterious effects to human health, living resources, or the quality of the marine environment.[92]

The council would be the most powerful IOS institution. The assembly, meeting only once every two years and in special sessions, would be limited to calling "the attention of the council to situations which it believes are likely to endanger the ecological integrity of IOS"[93] and to making "recommendations for the peaceful adjustment of any situation which it deems likely to impair the ecology of ocean space."[94] The secretariat would serve the chief administrative functions of the IOS institutions, reporting periodically to the council and inspecting the exploration and exploitation activities of any state in IOS.[95] It would also maintain a radioactive waste disposal register.[96] The international maritime court would exercise juridical competence, except over states, with respect to matters in IOS.[97] The council would have primary responsibility for harmonizing the actions of nations and maintaining the ecological, territorial, and jurisdictional integrity of natural resources in IOS.[98]

Should the council determine that some process would endanger the natural state of the marine environment or impair the ecological integrity of IOS, it would be empowered: (1) to publish a report containing a statement of the facts; (2) to make such recommendations as may appear necessary on reliable scientific advice to the coastal state or states concerned if the action occurred in national ocean space;[99] (3) to take such action within its powers as it deems necessary or desirable, including the regulation of dangerous practices or technologies and the prohibition or licensing of the disposal of harmful substances in IOS; and (4) to proclaim a regional or world ecological emergency in the event of imminent danger of serious contamination of extensive areas of IOS.[100] During a state of emergency, states within the region or all states in the world, as the case may be, whether or not members of the IOS institutions, would be required to promptly take such action for the preservation of the ocean space ecology as may be prescribed by the council.[101] To ensure compliance with its directions, the council could: (1) bring the matter before the international maritime court; (2) exclude offenders from participation in the equitable sharing of benefits derived from the exploitation of the natural resources of IOS; (3) exclude offenders from exploiting the natural resources of IOS; (4) exclude offenders from making use of IOS or the airspace above IOS for some or all purposes; or (5) call upon some or all members to ensure compliance with its decisions by such action as may be necessary, including the employment of naval and air forces.[102]

Critique

This writer's first impression of the Maltese draft from a pollution control perspective was that it was too comprehensively good to be true. It is so comprehensive that its very excellence may be its greatest weakness. No other official government draft approaches the Maltese draft as an idealized model for international environmental law; no other official government draft even explicitly recognizes the interdependence of ocean space and the undeniable fact that the oceans represent one of the earth's most delicately balanced ecological unities. While drawing on selected principles and articles of previous treaties, the Pardo proposal departs from the historical trends in a sweeping repudiation of the continental shelf doctrine and the traditional concept of freedom of the high seas, claiming that recent technological advances have rendered them obsolete. The world political community is harmonized in procrustean adaptations of power realities and weighted voting to exploit ocean resources while at the same time preserving and protecting the marine environment.

The major obvious difficulties of the Maltese draft would appear to be its broad scope. Many states regard the extension of territorial waters to 200 miles as an overly reckless and fatalistic concession to Latin American interests. The provisions for navigation through straits--twelve-mile zones <u>without</u> guarantees of unhampered passage[103]--run contrary to the U.S. and Soviet military interests.[104] By accommodating the most extreme demands for national jurisdiction and by neglecting to compromise the perceived vital national interests of certain states, the Maltese draft's viability as a pollution control model may be moot.

Even if these impediments were removed, the Maltese draft would be unacceptable to the international community. While the draft does allow time for certain evolutions,[105] the normal order of major developments is inverted. Regional arrangements for any or all treaty purposes would be established with consent of the council, after the convention entered into force. But most international experts view such arrangements as a necessary precondition rather than a product of the finalization of any global conventions.[106]

Different regions have different oceanographic conditions, different degrees of pollution, and different pollutants. Some, such as the Mediterranean and the Baltic, are approaching crisis pollution stages. Western Europe, Japan, and the United States are far more industrialized than developing African and Latin American states, and so are faced with different hazards. While pollutants eventually affect the total marine environment, regional differences and needs must be provided for in developing international standards and regulations. The Maltese draft could be made more realistic by incorporating a recognition of this evolutionary prerequisite.

By ceding pollution control jurisdiction to states in 200-mile wide belts, the Maltese draft might encourage de facto economically competitive situations in which the lax enforcement of pollution control regulations in one state for deliberate or unavoidable reasons might place an unacceptable burden on industry in another where enforcement is paramount. Pollution from oil development "would be very acceptable to lesser developed countries bringing to them as it would greater industrialization and economic growth." This economic competition situation could be avoided by providing institutional guarantees against lax enforcement of international pollution control standards. Coastal states could be required to prove enforcement capability by allocating a ratio of men, ships, and scientists to offshore zones and by permitting international experts to act as observers. In the absence of such guarantees, the council could administer the area "in trust."

Still, the Maltese draft provides an outstanding model of functional internationalism. The comprehensiveness of its approach, the flexibility and strength of its proposed sanctions, its recognition that emergency situations would have to be applied to all members of the world community, and its division of powers are key elements in preserving the global environment. At present it is not politically feasible, but in the future it may be environmentally necessary.

NOTES

1. UN General Assembly, International Law Commission, second session, Report of the ILC (Geneva, June 5-July 29, 1950), A/CN.4/34, p. 61.
2. Arthur M. Holcombe, chairman, Strengthening the United Nations, tenth report of the Committee to Study the Organization of Peace (New York: Harper, 1957), pp. 208-13.

3. See Clark Grenville and Louis B. Sohn, World Peace Through World Law (2nd rev. ed.; Cambridge, Mass.: Harvard University Press, 1962), p. 158.

4. Richard N. Gardner, Blueprint for Peace (New York: McGraw-Hill, 1966), pp. 145-46.

5. Clark M. Eicheberger, ed., New Dimensions for the United Nations, seventeenth report of the Committee to Study the Organization of Peace (Dobbs Ferry, N.Y.: Oceana, 1966), pp. 135-65.

6. See UN Doc A/C.1/PV. 1589, pp. 6-7, for original estimates; "Statement" delivered by Arvid Pardo, permanent representative of Malta to the United Nations in the Main Committee (Geneva, March 23, 1971).

7. See UN General Assembly Resolution 2750 (XXV) in UN Doc A/8097 (December 16, 1970).

8. See Hearings on Internationalization of the Seabed before the U.S. Congress, 1967, and an account of U.S. domestic lobbying in congressional debate in G. Weissberg, "International Law Meets the Short-term National Interest: The Maltese Proposal on the Seabed and Ocean Floor," International and Comparative Law Quarterly 18 (1969): 41-102.

9. Senate Resolution 92, 91st Cong. 1st Sess., p. 8, Article 13.

10. Ibid., p. 10, Article 16 (a) (v).

11. Ibid., p. 2, Article 16 (f)

12. Ibid., p. 13, Article 17 (5).

13. Ibid., p. 5, Article 24 (1).

14. Ibid., p. 20, Article 30 (a).

15. Ibid., p. 19, Article 28.

16. Ibid., p. 21, Article 31.

17. Claiborne Pell, "Ocean Space: Prospects and Proposals," draft report of the North Atlantic Assembly, Scientific and Technical Committee (Ottawa, Canada: International Secretariat, September 1969), p. 3.

18. Elizabeth Mann Borgese, The Ocean Regime: A Suggested Statute, a Center Occasional Paper (Santa Barbara, Calif.: Center for the Study of Democratic Institutions, October 1968), p. 3.

19. Ibid.

20. Ibid., p. 4.

21. Aaron Danzig draft treaty, Article VIII (New York: World Peace Through Law Center).

22. See Proceedings, Pacem in Maribus 1 and 2, 1970-71 (Santa Barbara, Calif.: Center for the Study of Democratic Institutions, 1970-71).

23. See draft statute in ibid. (1970), Article V, p. 11.

24. *Ibid.*, Article 6, p. 11.
25. *Ibid.*, Article III, p. 10.
26. *Ibid.*, Article IX, p. 14.
27. *Ibid.*, Article VIII, p. 13.
28. *Ibid.*
29. *Ibid.*, Article X, p. 16.
30. *Ibid.*, Article XIII, p. 18.
31. *Ibid.*, in "Comment," Article II, p. 23.
32. *Ibid.*
33. *Ibid.*, Article II, p. 24.
34. *Proceedings, Pacem in Maribus* (1971), *op. cit.*, p. 429.
35. UN Committee on the Peaceful Uses of the Sea Bed, "International Regime: Working Paper of the United Kingdom," A/AC.138/26 (August 5, 1970).
36. *Ibid.*
37. *Ibid.*, p. 3, Section 6a.
38. *Ibid.*, p. 2, Section 4.
39. *Ibid.*, Section 5ab.
40. *Ibid.*, Section 11bc.
41. See especially "Motion--the Seabed" and "World Ocean Regime Proposal," the *Parliamentary Debates* (Hansard) 313, no. 27 (London: HMSO, November 25, 1970), cols. 132, 152.
42. Convention for the Prevention of Marine Pollution by Dumping from Sea and Aircraft, UN General Assembly Doc A/AC.138/ SC. III/L.9 (March 13, 1972).
43. *Ibid.*, Part 1, Article 2.
44. *Ibid.*, Part 2, Article 3.
45. *Ibid.*, Article 8, p. 2.
46. *Ibid.*, Annex I, p. 8.
47. *Ibid.*, Annex II, p. 9.
48. *Ibid.*, Article 17, p. 4.
49. Untitled UN mimeo, A/AC.138/25 (August 3, 1970).
50. *Ibid.*
51. *Ibid.*
52. *Ibid.*
53. *Ibid.*
54. John R. Stevenson, "Statement" at Hearings before the U.S. Senate Subcommittee on Oceans and Atmosphere (October 3, 1972), p. 3.
55. UN Doc A/AC.138/25, *op. cit.*, Article I:2.
56. *Ibid.*, Article 67: Procedure.
57. *Ibid.*, Article 68.
58. *Ibid.*, Article 11:4.
59. *Ibid.*, Article 23.
60. *Ibid.*

61. Ibid., Article 59.

62. Ibid., Appendix C:10.

63. Unpublished mimeo, "Working Paper on Competence to Establish Standards for the Control of Vessel Source Pollution," submitted to UN Committee on the Peaceful Uses of the Sea-Bed by the United States, April 2, 1973.

64. John R. Stevenson, "Statement" before the UN Committee on the Peaceful Uses of the Sea-Bed, Subcommittee III, August 1972.

65. Ibid.

66. Ibid.

67. John R. Stevenson, "Department Discusses Progress Towards 1973 Conference on the Law of the Sea," Department of State Bulletin, May 8, 1972, p. 672.

68. Ibid., p. 677.

69. The Secretary of State's Advisory Committee on the 1972 UN Conference on the Human Environment, Stockholm and Beyond (Washington, D.C.: May 1972), pp. 129-46.

70. Lewis M. Alexander, Letter to Senator Hollings dated November 3, 1972.

71. For example, the efforts of various governments to halt French nuclear tests on Mururoa Island in the South Pacific, July 1973.

72. Robert B. Krueger, "International and National Regulation of Pollution from Off-shore Oil Production," in Donald Hood, ed., Impingement of Man on the Oceans (New York: Wiley Interscience, 1971), p. 612.

73. Daniel Wilkes, "Canada's Arctic Regulations," Journal of Maritime Law and Commerce, pp. 605-06.

74. Lewis M. Alexander, op. cit., p. 88.

75. Maltese Draft Ocean Space Treaty, UN Doc A/AC.138/53 (August 23, 1971).

76. See remarks of Elizabeth M. Borgese in Proceedings, Pacem in Maribus (1971), op. cit., pp. 419-31.

77. Ibid., Part V, "A Constitution for the Oceans," pp. 410-89.

78. Maltese Draft Ocean Space Treaty, op. cit., p. 6.

79. Ibid., p. 27.

80. Ibid., pp. 31-32, Chapter XI, Article 48.

81. Ibid., p. 35, Article 55. This provision would extend certain provisions of Article 17 of the 1958 Geneva Territorial Sea Convention.

82. Ibid., Article 57, p. 37.

83. Ibid., Article 59: 1a, p. 37.

84. Ibid., Article 62, p. 39.

85. Ibid., Article 94:1, p. 51.

86. Ibid., Article 66, p. 41.

87. See General Assembly Resolution 2749 (XXV), para. 1.

88. Maltese Draft Ocean Space Treaty, op. cit., Article 74, p. 42, which is similar to Article 9 of the U.S. draft convention (A/8021, Annex V) and Article 12 of the Tanzanian draft (A/AC.138/33).

89. Maltese Draft Ocean Space Treaty, op. cit., Article 72, p. 42.

90. Ibid., Article 77, p. 43. (This represents a slight modification of Senator Pell's Article 5, Article VI of the Danzig draft, and Article III b9 of the Borgese statute.)

91. Ibid., Article 81, p. 45.

92. Ibid., Article 82, p. 46.

93. Ibid., Article 98:3, p. 53.

94. Ibid., Article 100, p. 53.

95. Ibid., Article 165, p. 74.

96. Ibid.

97. Ibid., Article 161, p. 72.

98. Ibid., Article 125, p. 61.

99. Ibid., Article 155, p. 71.

100. Ibid., Article 156, p. 71.

101. Ibid., Article 155, p. 71.

102. Ibid., Articles 149-150, pp. 68-69.

103. See Louis B. Sohn, "Comments on Dr. Arvid Pardo's Draft Treaty," in Proceedings, Pacem in Maribus (1971), op. cit., p. 463.

104. Friedheim, op. cit.

105. Maltese Draft Ocean Space Treaty, op. cit., Chapter XXVIII, pp. 79-85.

106. Richard A. Falk, "Towards a World Order Respectful of the Global Ecosystem," Environmental Affairs 1, no. 2 (June 1971): 251-65. The following concurred in private interviews with the author: Mario Ruivo (FAO-fisheries), Gerald Moore (FAO-legal counsel), T. E. Carroz (FAO-legal counsel), Thomas Busha (IMCO-legal counsel), Daniel Wilkes (URI-master of marine affairs).

8

POLICY IMPLICATIONS

"When key pollutants have been identified, their effects ascertained, their sources found, their rates of accumulation calculated, their routes traced, and their final sinks or reservoirs located, the question of what to do about them will remain."[1] Assuming a general public disposition to eliminate or diminish pollution, the 1970 MIT (Massachusetts Institute of Technology) study of critical environmental problems sought to identify the how and the consequences of such action. It concluded that an objective analysis of the implications of change must acknowledge differences in value judgments and man-environment concepts but must also presume a shift in values toward a more complete understanding of the consequences of public and private choice. That study, like this one, sought to identify the "external" or "social costs" of pollution, which are not taken into account in the ordinary business calculations of income and expense. Such calculations are important in discussing policy alternatives. The social implications of marine pollution control also involve considerations of the public or collective good,[2] and determinations of who benefits at what costs.

The value judgments of this "objective analysis" define the international collective good as environmental quality sufficient to maintain a stable, healthy ecosystem and a healthy human existence; international diseconomies are defined as pollutants that are hazardous, cumulative, and persistent. But what is desirable for one global region may mean disaster for another; what is necessary for long-term global survival may be economically impossible for certain regions alone to bear. If the existing patterns of marine pollution are to be altered, the distribution of costs will have to be allocated according to formulas other than population and sovereign states.

Generally, environmental research includes the following goals:

. Simply to know, on a continuing basis, what in fact is going on.

. To determine the likely effects of present trends, and to establish tolerances.

. To develop alternatives to or modification of current practices when necessary.

. To establish hard data on the costs and benefits of alternative courses of action for political decision.[3]

These objectives are common to international conferences on environmental problems and have partially served as the objectives of this study. Preceding chapters have reviewed trends in pollutant quantity and distribution and in the international law for its control. Certain tolerance levels have been determined and certain absorption "budgets" projected. While modifications of certain practices are possible, "hard" data on alternative costs and benefits are difficult if not impossible to determine, except in the short term. Long-term predictions are speculative and in some instances dangerous. The short-term costs of substituting nonpersistent pesticides for DDT, of recycling metals, of more efficient exhaust emission controls for automobiles, of reducing offshore drilling or improving shore reception facilities for oil tankers--all these can be determined But the long-range consequences of inaction are impossible to establish. "If-then" scenarios are useful in arousing public interest, but they confound the decision-making process.

Decision-makers are accustomed to incomplete knowledge; this is always the case.[4] The entire political process is accustomed to decisions in the face of uncertainty on the basis of a preponderance of the evidence or substantial probabilities or a reasonable consensus of informed judgment.[5] It is neither necessary nor feasible to postpone recommendations for action until scientific certainty can be achieved.

The following policy implications for controlling the major marine pollutants derive from group studies and the author's observations.

OIL AND THE HYDROCARBONS

A number of existing and foreseeable control techniques are possible:

1. Universal adoption of the "load-on-top" technique coupled with the development of efficient oily water separators and shore reception facilities.

2. Safer standards in the design and construction of oil tankers, including the use of small and well-shielded interior tanks compartmentalized for protection against ruptures.

3. Establishment of worldwide traffic separation schemes to prevent collisions similar to those used for aircraft control.

4. The rigorous enforcement of safer standards for offshore drilling operations; prohibition of drilling in areas particularly sensitive to earthquakes or pollution.

5. Strict and unlimited liability tolerance in areas under coastal jurisdiction and/or a rearrangement of absurd "flag of convenience" arrangements.

6. Tax and subsidy incentives to encourage or force the recycling of crankcase oil and used industrial oil.

7. Prohibition of discharges from bilges and a requirement of holding tanks on all vessels.

8. Public support of research on biodegrading bacteria.[6]

The benefits of limiting or lowering the amount of hydrocarbons entering the marine environment would be to improve esthetic and recreational beach quality, to preserve marine bird and fish species vital to ocean ecology, to increase untainted shellfish availability and other seafoods for human or animal consumption, and to maintain a healthy estuarine zone vital to the reproduction of many marine species. The major costs would be an increase in the price of oil or a dependency on foreign sources for most industrial nations. The price might also include the cost of monitoring and enforcing water quality standards and establishing a fund to pay for oil spill damage to property and environment, as well as clean-up costs.

RADIOACTIVE WASTES

The production of radioactive waste under existing fission technology is unavoidable; methods have been devised to concentrate and reduce its volume (calcinator technique) and to reuse it in fuel regeneration processes (breeder reactors). But concentration techniques do not reduce specific activity of material requiring disposal. Breeder reactors require less fuel, but they may present even greater risks than conventional reactors.

Nuclear power generation faces two environmental imperatives: to develop safe and economical storage sites for projected wastes or to discontinue development. The use of the sea as a "convenient" waste disposal site persists for states with few or no alternative land disposal facilities (such as Japan and Western Europe). The Soviet Union has adequate land disposal storage sites. The United States discontinued licensing sea disposal in 1971 and made economic disposal facilities available in abandoned salt mines. The change in U.S. policy resulted from a convenient coincidence of economics and environmental concern, with the AEC maintaining that sea disposal is still a convenient and "safe" method. If the major powers conclude that further sea disposal is environmentally undesirable, it will be incumbent upon them to offer or rent space to those who have none; the United States has done this under the Atoms for Peace Program. Also, international subsidies might be devised to provide an equal distribution of the economic burden such a change in policy might require.

The benefits of reducing or eliminating the sea disposal of radioactive wastes are impossible to assess in the long run; they range from future use of living marine resources that otherwise might become contaminated to the maintenance of an oceanic ecosystem that might be upset or destroyed through genetic or somatic damage. The costs involve the development of disposal alternatives, the loss of capital investment and projected nuclear power production of fission plants, as well as the increased costs of relying on other energy inputs.

PESTICIDES

Continued use of DDT and other persistent pesticides has reduced populations and increased reproductive failures of fish-eating birds. Certain marine food fish have declined in productivity and exhibited increased accumulation levels of DDT and other pesticides in their tissue. Pesticide degradation rates in the marine environment are unknown, although half-lives involve years and decades. There are no reliable estimates and no direct measures of the concentrations and effects of DDT in the open oceans.

Drastic reductions in the use of DDT and other persistent substances without the concurrent provision of less persistent subsidized alternatives would present some very serious problems in disease control and crop yield maintenance in underdeveloped countries and in the

production of cotton crops in developed countries such as
the United States. Several developing countries claim
that outright bans without subsidized substitutes would
mean genocide for their peoples, not only through disease
but also from famine. Many of the super crops developed
in the "green revolution" require pesticide protection to
flourish. Replacement of DDT in the U.S. cotton crop
would add 3 to 5 percent of the cost of production, or
1 cent to the final product of a commodity already in a
severe price squeeze due to competition from synthetics.

HEAVY METALS

Heavy metals must be removed as close to their point
of origin as possible to prevent marine pollution. Once
dissolved and dispersed, their removal at central sewage
treatment plants is impractical. Most techniques for removing heavy metal ions from wastes through precipitation
or ion exchange involve inexpensive chemical operations.
Effluents from mercury cell chlor-alkali plants, one of
the major sources of mercury, can be completely cleared
of the metal by using settling basins and recycle systems,
although effluent control for small operators and laboratories is more difficult to establish. Many operators
are unaware that their effluent contains heavy metals
that are toxic. To reduce discharges, authorities could:
1. Publicize the toxicity of heavy metals and establish food content standards; levels have already been
determined by the U.S. Food and Drug Administration for
both lead and mercury.
2. Establish and enforce water quality standards.
3. Register users of heavy metal salts and mercury
and monitor their effluents.
4. Obtain regional and global data on the amount of
each metal being introduced into the environment.
Regulating the flow of heavy metals into the marine
environment would reduce the incidence of poisoning from
contaminated fish, oysters, and other living resources.
It would also improve the erratic performance of many
sewage treatment plants whose processes employ ion ex-
changes, and improve rivers and estuaries.
The costs of heavy metal controls do not appear
large. Expenses for establishing, monitoring, and enforcing water quality standards could be obtained through
direct taxes on the sources of the effluents or from general tax revenues. The costs of recycling metals could
be passed on to the industries' consumers or borne by

general taxpayers in the form of subsidies or capital improvement allowances.

NUTRIENTS

Many estuaries are semienclosed basins prone to accumulations of riverborne sediment and wastes, as well as the natural discharge of nutrients and solids from river and rain. Nitrogen in various forms is supplied in nearly equal amounts by sewage treatment plants, storm water runoff, and subsurface seawater.

There are a number of techniques available to control these emissions:

1. Reclaiming and recycling nutrients in areas of high concentrations, such as sewage treatment plants and feedlots.

2. Restricting the flow of industrial wastes to sewage systems so that toxic wastes do not interfere with nutrient recovery and recycling.

3. Applying phosphate removal techniques to industrial discharges.

4. Reducing or eliminating phosphates in detergents, replacing them with nonbiotoxic, biodegradable agents with suitable detergency.

5. Improving institutional structures responsible for defining, monitoring, and maintaining water quality standards over large areas.

The reduction of nutrients and phosphate levels in the marine environment would reduce the exhaustion of dissolved oxygen in bottom waters, which kills all normal benthic organisms. It would reduce the eutrophication rate, improve the esthetics, and enhance the recreational quality of many lakes, rivers, and estuaries.

The major costs of reducing nutrient levels in the marine environment would involve agricultural education work and the construction of nutrient recycling systems; establishment, monitoring, and enforcement of water quality standards; and removal or replacement of the polyphosphate detergents. Treatment costs for 80 to 90 percent removal run about 5 (U.S.) cents per 1,000 gallons, or 1 to 2 (U.S.) dollars per capita per year.

OTHER POLLUTANTS

Other marine pollutants also require timely international action. These include the disposition of obsolete military munitions, especially chemical and biological warfare agents. Dismantling centers have been constructed at storage sites and as mobile units. Their cost represents only a small proportion of the original production outlay. International agreement could provide for such centers and declare a moratorium on the production of indestructible munitions.

Thermal pollution and municipal wastes also pose long-term hazards for specific regions. Reducing or eliminating their release in the marine environment involves fundamental social change more than any specific control technique.[7] Heat emissions can be reduced (but not eliminated) through more efficient generating processes or atmospheric transfer via cooling towers. The social costs of limiting general wastes involve changes in lifestyle and the rationing of energy.

Reducing or eliminating the amount of toxic substances that reaches the ocean requires national and international assessments of the relationship between economic growth and environmental quality. Growth requires energy, and energy production is dependent on petroleum combustion and the fission of atomic piles. Growth also requires agricultural production and healthy populations; DDT and certain pesticides are needed by certain countries to maintain both. Energy production and artificial agricultural techniques cause environmental disruptions and ecological damage, so societies must evaluate the costs and benefits of growth versus environmental quality. Experience has proven that less developed countries will emphasize growth while developed countries will begin to focus on the environment. But the scientific evidence suggests that these tradeoffs can no longer be left to unilateral determination; the survival of the ocean's ecosystem is dependent on international cooperation.

CONCLUSION

All life on this earth is dependent on a viable marine ecosystem. The oceans provide our oxygen, our water, our temperate climates, and our food. Without them the Earth would be a wasteland.

All human activity affects the balance of life in the oceans. The cumulative effect of every interference, no matter how insignificant individually, is liable to produce a crown of thorns. Therefore, no major decision should be made without recognizing the interdependent quality of the marine environment and all possible impacts.

183

International political processes have not yet recognized ecological imperatives. National security and
economic development considerations continue to dominate
most forums. The problem is basically one of perception:
Communicating the need is as important as developing the
means for controlling marine pollution.

The most serious and immediate threats to ocean
ecology are the most difficult to regulate. There is no
international and very little national control over toxic
metals, radioactive wastes, chemical and biological warfare agents, polychlorinated biphenyls, and persistent
pesticides that reach the sea. There is no system for
subsidizing nonpolluting alternatives. There is no in-
centive to sacrifice development for long-term environmental quality.

Traditional treaty techniques are only marginally
suited to meeting the technical requirements of effective
ecomanagement and the flexible response demanded by accelerated technological change. Unanimity fails to meet
the special needs of certain states. Canada's unilateral
extension of pollution jurisdiction in response to weak
provisions in the Oil Pollution Convention amendments is
one example of the failure and inability to deal with regional differences. The implications of biosphere protection efforts extend beyond conventional international
agreement; national sovereignty must err on the side of
the environment or be relinquished to an international
authority.

While there do not as yet exist any ideal models for
standards setting, a majority of states already participate in international efforts involving standards for a
variety of subjects.[8] Many of these make common practice
of separating technical standards from basic treaty requirements, thereby facilitating timely revisions by
avoiding lengthy formal amendment procedures. National
enabling legislation is ensured through proper language
in the treaty and through reporting, critical review, or
inspection provisions. Originally conceived as a simpli-
fied method of treaty amendment (permissible under Article
40 of the Vienna Convention on the Law of Treaties), these
arrangements may be adaptable to environmental purposes.

Until recently, the traditional view of the democratic political process (on which the United Nations is
nominally based) as a power system based on intergroup
relationships[9] has been justified by the ability of special interest groups to influence their governments'
ocean policies. Mineral exploiters, fishermen, and

military strategists have been the animating forces of ocean policy formulation. Governments have largely limited themselves to referee roles by arbitrating and mediating among these interest groups.

This power system is changing, for national policies have been profoundly altered by three factors: the influence of foreign policy, the "future orientation" of society, and the increasing role of technical decision-making.[10] Foreign policy is beginning to be shaped in accord with great power and ideological interests, and not primarily in response to domestic group interests. Technocratic rationality, as distinguished from political bargaining, has become a highly important factor in national decision-making on issues of international security. Rational environmental controls require the same kind of expert objectivity.

The diffusion of marine pollution control programs throughout the UN system, the proliferation of "alphabet-soup" acronym projects to monitor and research pollution effects, and the substantial redundancy in different forums is symptomatic of a general lack of international political will to effectively regulate marine pollution.

The sectoral orientation and limited pollution jurisdiction of separate UN agencies under the "manageable packages" concept has limited general public threat perception and, hence, movement for greater control. Consolidations of environmental policy-making and enforcement agencies (at local, regional, and national levels) have provided focal points for environmental reform groups and regulation clarifications for industry. International agency reorganization for these purposes would have the same effects.[11]

Of the three international forums with international law-making capability, the United Nations (Stockholm) Conference on Human Environment and its secretariat are best structured to consider any and all environmental problems. The conference was designed to include discussion on three action levels: future planning, near-future action preparations, and immediate action proposals. The conference favored the establishment of a standing secretariat with strong functional links to international scientific advisory bodies, to provide a discussion forum and encourage future environmental conferences or special ad hoc meetings.

The IMCO and Law of the Sea conferences have not been designed to produce comprehensive regulation. IMCO is a shipping-transportation forum despite its internal environmental efforts; conferences under its sponsorship are therefore limited to discussion of regulating pollutants emanating from vessels. Regulating emissions or disposals from single sources without examining alternative impacts only transforms the problem. If industry is blocked from disposing waste from vessels, it has only to construct coastal outfalls. The pollutant is not stopped; the source is just changed.

The Law of the Sea Conference is too complicated by other issues to produce effective environmental treaty provisions. By tackling the problems of mineral exploitation, fishing, military security, and transportation in separate compartments, nation-states appear headed for a deadlock in legal negotiations. Governmental efforts to reconstruct the law of the sea and to establish ocean regimes are based primarily on resource management-development and national military security. Unless priorities are revised, it is unlikely that adequate standards and effective marine pollution control mechanisms will come out of the Law of the Sea Conference.

The ocean is the key to survival, the pivotal base of all life and atmospheric cycles. Therefore, the overriding objective of a public ocean policy, whether national or global, must be to maintain the viability of the ecosystem, for without it there are no other considerations.[12] The first order of public policy for the ocean must be environmental protection and management.

The responsibility and impetus for establishing this relatively new domestic and foreign policy cannot be relegated to traditional policy-making institutions and processes. Neither the marketplace of interest-group liberalism nor the rigid capital acquisition at any cost orientation of socialist economies provides the necessary "public good" input on national levels required for long-term environmental protection. These approaches are even less protective on international levels. To govern the oceans--as opposed to "snatch and squat" acquiescence-- an agreement is needed that will conform to the welfare of the whole world community without being inconsistent with the short-term perceived interests of the most important nations.[13]

The major defect of most UN seabed discussions is that they tend to proceed as if the sea itself were not there. Many delegates talk as though the seabed could be isolated and governed by legislation without regard to the fact that it is covered by water. Most draft treaties have referred to a need for conserving and protecting the environment, but these references are usually of a very weak and secondary character. What the proposals do have in common is the assumed right to exploit.

One way to break out of the legal deadlock that has begun to characterize official law of the sea convocations is an environmental approach. If negotiations were to start with the environment, instead of putting it last, nations would be more likely to find solutions for their separate problems within the context of established consensus. This approach means starting from the principle that it is in man's own best interests to preserve and improve his marine environment and to establish a general purpose regime with powers to regulate all activities in ecological, instead of political, zones. All activities would be permitted and controlled by one principle: whether they preserve or improve the environment. Activities would be encouraged if they did serve environmental interests; permitted subject to strict control if damage is slight; and prohibited--except when significant general advantage can be proved--if damage is serious.

A number of developments on the national and international level encourage such a policy. If nothing else, international environmental conferences encourage the formation of national environment agencies and organizations responsible for developing national positions. These agencies and organizations provide a central focus for the development of new professionals sensitive to the relations between the processes of production, distribution, and consumption on the one hand, and the processes of pollution on the other. Their training incorporates a disposition to explore all possibilities of technology and organization in the search for an optimal balance. Individual contributions from this group are not immediately realized because of present political compromise. But they will be critical over time as options for compromise are reduced.

These gatherings also enhance the ability of existing international organizations to appreciate the full significance of global marine pollution and to adjust their internal directions toward the functional roles they may be asked to assume in the future. Because of resource constraints, limited staff, and the need for consultation, international organizations have found it useful to coordinate their scientific and research efforts in the field of marine pollution. There is a distinct need for more scientific advisory systems, like GESAMP, which meet more often and exert institutionalized influence on decision-making. It is in the sphere of collection, organization, and analysis of essential data that the prospects are best for meeting the burden of demonstration and persuasion needed to move the international political process.[14]

In the immediate future the functional agencies will be most effective in providing assistance and advice to regional enforcement bodies similar to those now being developed for the North, Baltic, and Mediterranean seas. As a general rule, the higher the degree of economic and political integration, the greater the possibility of strict uniform controls. The 1972 Oslo Convention for the Prevention of Marine Pollution exemplifies the possibilities in integrated regions.

However, certain pollutants of immediate and dangerous impact require immediate international control agreements. The time required for regional mechanisms to evolve into global systems is too long to permit these materials to continue to enter the marine environment unregulated. National regulation of land source pollutants must be internationally harmonized. High on the list of those requiring immediate regulation are the persistent clorinated hydrocarbons, polychlorinated biphenyls, heavy metals, and radioactive contaminants. These pollutants are accumulated and concentrated by marine organisms and passed up the food chain to higher trophic levels. Minimal controls for these pollutants should be globally absolute, with provision for more stringent regional deviation. Subsidies for substitutes should be provided to developing countries by the international community. The most equitable income scheme to support such a world community "public good" could be assessed on each nation according to ability to pay.

The development of an international environmental policy involves four phases: (1) identifying pollutants and their effects; (2) ranking them in order of priority from both human and environmental points of view; (3) determining the technical ways and means of controlling or preventing their release; and (4) inducing universal and regional commitments to action. Many of the contaminants discussed in this study have passed through the first three stages. Commitments to control oil are limited, but they exist. However, international agreement on issues with major economic impact is likely to become more rather than less difficult to achieve.[15] The growing realization by governments, especially those of developing countries, of the interdependence and interpenetration of societies is likely to make them increasingly jealous of the prerogatives they retain. But "While nations cling to national sovereignty . . . science has created a functional international society, whether anyone likes it or not."[16] To prevent anarchical environmental degradation, political leaders must be made to recognize:

. That freedom of national action and the inviolability of borders have long since lost so much of their traditional meaning.

. That the resource size of most nation-states is incommensurate with the requirements of modern technology.

. That international organizations must fill a more important role than simply amplifying big power goals.[17]

Inducing governments to recognize the merits of the environmental approach in international affairs, to widen their perceptions of self-interest, and to recast their proposals and priorities for the control of marine pollution is exceedingly difficult but not impossible to bring about. It will involve a fundamental educational process coupled with a tremendous public relations effort if it is to be accomplished through the democratic processes. Adaptation to the ecological age presupposes new structures of power and massive reform of existing systems. The first law of ecological politics is that there exists an inverse relationship between the interval of time available for adaptive change and the likelihood and intensity of violence, trauma, and coercion accompanying the process of adaptation.[18] Put simply--the sooner, the better, especially if the survival of democratic society is a positive goal to be secured. The alternatives are ecological catastrophe, dictatorial rule, or conspiratorial task forces to pick up the pieces.[19]

Individuals can participate in world-order activism by designing new systems,[20] adopting new lifestyles, acquiring knowledge and spreading it to others. Responsible political action depends upon knowledge and the selection of optimal courses of action. Power and influence, on the other hand, are basically group or money functions. Both must be developed to obtain results.

If we go on thinking in terms of nation-states, the world is doomed to disaster. The world is one, both humanly and environmentally. Our arrangements must express this truth both in the environment and in human organization.

1. The application of the theory of collective goods to political problems stems from the work of Mancur Olson, Jr., in The Logic of Collective Action: Political Goods and the Theory of Groups (Cambridge, Mass.: Harvard University Press, 1965) and to international politics from Olson and R. Zechhouser in "An Economic Theory of Alliances," Review of Economics and Statistics 48, no. 3 (August 1966): 266-79.

For a discussion of political integration theory, see Leon N. Lindberg and Stuart A. Scheingold in Europe's Would-Be Policy: Patterns of Change in the European Community (Englewood Cliffs, N.J.: Prentice-Hall, 1970), pp. 155-57, and the special issue of International Organization 24, no. 4 (Autumn 1971).

2. Bruce M. Russett and John D. Sullivan, "Collective Goods and International Organization," International Organization 25, no. 4 (Autumn 1971): 846.

3. Eugene B. Skolnikoff, "International Functional Implications of Future Technology," International Affairs 25, no. 2 (1971): 274.

4. Richard A. Carpenter, "Expectations of the Decision Maker," in W. Matthews, ed., Man's Impact on Terrestrial and Oceanic Ecosystems (Cambridge, Mass.: MIT Press, 1971), p. 474.

5. Matthews, ed., op. cit., p. 471.

6. See, for example, "Oil Eaters," Time, May 21, 1973, p. 60, for a description of a fast multiplying bacterial strain called RAG-1.

7. See particularly the extensive statement and written documents submitted by Barry Commoner at Hearings before the Subcommittee on Oceans and Atmosphere on International Conference on Ocean Pollution, October 8 and November 8, 1971, pp. 56-119.

8. Paolo Contini and Peter H. Sand, "Methods to Expedite Environment Protection: International Ecostandards," American Journal of International Law 66, no. 1 (January 1972): 37-60.

9. See, for example, Charles E. Merriam, Political Power (New York: McGraw Hill, 1934), pp. 18-23; V. O. Key, Jr., Politics, Parties and Pressure Groups (New York: Thomas Crowell, 1947), pp. 6-9.

10. Daniel Bell, "Notes on the Post Industrial Society, II," The Public Interest, Spring 1967, pp. 106-8.

11. See, for example, the proposals of George F. Kennan (Foreign Affairs 1970) and Lynton K. Caldwell, In

<u>Defense of Earth</u> (Bloomington, Indiana: University of
Illinois Press, 1972).

   12.   E. W. Seabrook Hull, "Toward a Public Policy on
the Ocean," in Donald W. Hood, ed., <u>Impingement of Man On
the Oceans</u> (New York: Wiley, 1972), p. 657.

   13.   Richard A. Falk and A. G. Millbank, "Inability
of Traditional Forms of Political Order to Adapt to Modern Problems of International Pollution," in <u>Proceedings</u>
of the International and Interstate Regulation of Water
Pollution, sponsored by the Columbia University School of
Law, printed in <u>Columbia Journal of Transnational Law</u>,
1970, pp. 11-17.

   14.   Report of the MIT (Massachusetts Institute of
Technology) Study on Critical Environmental Problems
(SCEP) (Cambridge, Mass.:   MIT Press), p. 249.

   15.   Eugene B. Skolnikoff, "Science and Technology:
The Implications for International Institutions," <u>Inter-
national Organization</u> 25, no. 4 (Autumn 1971):   763.

   16.   Skolnikoff, <u>op. cit</u>.

   17.   E. B. Skolnikoff, "The International Functional
Implications of Future Technology," <u>Journal of International Affairs</u> 25, no. 2 (1971):   266.

   18.   Richard Falk, <u>This Endangered Planet</u> (New York:
Random House, 1971), p. 353.

   19.   <u>Ibid</u>., p. 365.

   20.   See, for example, George F. Kennan, "To Prevent
a World Wasteland," <u>Foreign Affairs</u> 1, no. 2 (1970); E. W.
Seabrook Hull and Albert W. Koers, "Introduction to a
Convention on the International Environmental Protection
Agency," Occasional Paper No. 12 (Kingston: University
of Rhode Island, Law of the Sea Institute, September 1971).

EFFECTS OF KEY PROVISIONS OF THE CANADIAN
ARCTIC WATERS ANTI-POLLUTION PACKAGE

By Daniel Wilkes, Department of Political
Science and Master of Marine Affairs
Program, University of Rhode Island

Recent acts to control Canada's water passages in
the Arctic have been ascribed to a plethora of motives.
In analyzing the enabling provisions of these important
acts, which are set out below, the ecological crisis that
lay behind them must not be forgotten. In August and
September 1969, SS Manhattan proved that the Northwest
Passage could be used to carry oil from Alaska's North
Slope, Mackenzie District, or the Queen Elizabeth Islands
to southern refineries. This route would result in substantial savings over other means of transport, would
quickly bring oil to market, and, together with political
developments in the Middle East, was certain to stimulate
oil development on the Canadian islands. Because it
takes only about 18 months to build a large tanker, decisions on contracts that involved Arctic specifications
lay in the very near future.

It was at this point that a high-level Canadian government group put together what became Bill C-202, the
act "to prevent pollution of areas of the arctic waters
adjacent to the mainland and islands of the Canadian
arctic," and Bill C-203, the amendment to the Territorial
Sea and Fishing Zones Act, which made most passages "territorial" waters by extending the territorial limit to 12
miles. On April 8, 1970, both bills were introduced by
the Government; they were passed by the lower house in
June and received royal assent in August 1970.

Canadian intentions to protect the Arctic ecology
had been evident for some time. For instance, it was a
significant reason advanced for the "Sector Claim" to
Canadian sovereignty over all islands within lines extended from her east and west borders to the North Pole.
Indeed, the first--and still the most significant--imple-
mentation of that claim has been the insistence on federal

licensing and control of hunting there, including protection of polar bears and other threatened species.

   More recently, Canada worked hard to try to get a
strong emphasis on preventing, rather than "paying for,"
oil pollution at sea at the Brussels meeting of Inter-
Governmental Maritime Consultative Organization (IMCO)
called on that subject. The sharp rebuffs Canada received
on that point could be said to have shown her officials
that the wildlife of the Arctic snows and seas would not
be protectable in time if the acts outlined below were
held up for IMCO action.

Effects of Key Provisions of Bill C-202

Provision	Effect	Section*
They extend	to "Arctic waters," north of lat. 60° N, east of long. 141° W, west of a line equidistant between Canada and Greenland, within 100 nautical miles of shore; and to continental shelves or other substrata Canada has the "right to exploit."	3(1) 3(2)
They include	territorial seas 12 miles from shore or from any straight base-lines and all channels of any kind through the Canadian Arctic islands.	TSFZA 3(1) as amended**
They exclude	parts of Canada south of lat. 60° N, waters within the "Polar Sector" more than 100 miles from land (except, arguably, for civil liability for pollution of the continental shelf more than 100 miles from land), and inland waters.	3(1) 3(2) 6(1)(a)

---

   *Section references are to the Arctic Waters Pollu-
tion Prevention Act of 1970.
   **This section reference is to the Territorial Sea and
Fishing Zones Act, 1965, 13-14 Eliz II, c 22, as amended.

Provision	Effect	Section
They forbid	the disposal or allowance of waste of any kind, unless authorized by new regulations or by regulations of the Canada Water Act. Waste is any sub-stance . . . detrimental to the use of Arctic waters . . . by men or animals, fish and plants useful to men, including detri-mentally altered water.	4(1), (2), and (3) 2(h)
They apply	to anyone who deposits waste . . . in Arctic waters, or on mainland or islands north of lat. 60° N, whether or not waste enters those waters or leads to waste that enters them, and whether or not it is done by a person or his agent, deliberately, carelessly, or without fault, and whether or not already deposited or simply in danger of being deposited.	4(1) and (3) 7(2) 5(1) and (2) 7(1) 5(1)
They render liable	to civil suit natural resource explorers, exploiters, or de-velopers on any land adjacent to or under Arctic waters; anyone carrying on any undertaking north of lat. 60° N; owners of ships, including charter parties; and owners of cargoes on ships for pollution damage to Arctic waters. Liability is for "actual loss" or damage and to the gov-ernment of Canada for its reason-able expenses. Suits must be brought within two years after deposit could be expected to be known. Liability is assessed by the share of damage and by the expense or loss to the degree that conduct contributed to it.	6(1)(a) 6(1)(b) 6(1)(c) 6(2)(c) 6(1)(c) 6(1)(e) 6(4) 7(1)

Provision	Effect	Section
Governor-in-Council can	make anyone post a bond, for which he is liable if he owns a ship navigating through Arctic safety zones;	8 8(1)(d)
	if he owns cargo on such a ship; if he explores, develops, or exploits a resource there; if he carries on a waste-producing activity there; if he builds or alters works connected with such activities;	8(1)(a) 8(1)(b) 8(1)(c)
and can	regulate any waste-producing or waste-threatening activity, ship, or cargo;	9, 11, 12
and can	make anyone submit plans for waste-producing works, and forbid them from building or altering them, or place necessary conditions on building them;	10(1) 10(2)(b) 10(2)(a)
and can	require ships to meet Canadian requirements as to hull and fuel tank construction (including strength, double hulls, compartments); as to aids to navigation and telecommunications and their maintenance schedules; as to kind of propelling power and steering and stabilizing gear; as to how many crew to man the ship, with Canadian-qualified pilots and lookouts; as to maximum cargo per type and how stowed and with supplies to repair cargo leaks and clean up waste from cargo accidents; as to freeboard allowed and load line markings; as to amounts of fuel, water, supplies, charts, tide tables, and navigation books carried; as to certificates to show compliance.	12(1)(a)(i) 12(1)(a)(ii) 12(1)(a)(iii) 12(1)(a)(iv) 12(1)(a)(v) 12(1)(a)(vi) 12(1)(a)(vii) and (viii) 12(3)

Provision	Effect	Section
Canada may prohibit	ships that do not meet above requirements or go without required pilots, ice navigators, or icebreakers, or go in closed periods or when prohibiting ice conditions exist.	12(1)(a) 12(1)(b) 12(1)(c)
Governor-in-Council can	destroy, move, or sell any ship or cargo to offset proceeds of sale against federal expenses if distress is "reasonably believed likely to deposit waste."	13(1) 13(2)
Pollution prevention officers may be empowered	at reasonable times to enter areas where waste is or may be resulting (except in ships or private dwellings) to sample waste, to order documents to be produced, to inspect work on waste-producing plants; and in relation to safety zones to board ships in such zones to check compliance, and to direct movements of ships in or near such zones if there is reasonable suspicion of non-compliance and if interests of safety require such action; and to order, if there is substantial waste or imminent danger of it, ships in the area to report their positions, to help control or clean up waste, and to order the owner of waste, his agent, or anyone there to furnish reasonable information.	14, 15(1) 15(1)(b) 15(1)(c) 15(2) 15(3)(a) 15(3)(b)(i) and (ii) 15(3)(b)(iii) 15(3)(c)(i) 15(3)(c)(ii) 16

Provision	Effect	Section
Penalties on summary conviction	for making or permitting an unauthorized deposit are up to $5,000/person/day or $100,000/ship and/or seizure and forfeiture of ship and cargo;	18 23(1) 24(1)
	for failing, when required, to report a waste deposit are up to $25,000 and/or seizure or forfeiture; for failing to submit plans or to post bonds or the equivalent are up to $25,000; for building or altering work or deviating from plan are up to $25,000;	19(1)(a) 23(1), 24(1) 19(1)(c) 19(1)(b) 19(1)(d)
	for ships navigating in zones against rules are up to $25,000 and/or seizure or forfeiture; or for failure to follow orders of pilot, when reasonable, or of pollution prevention officer to stay outside of zone or to move into a zone or for non-compliance, danger of waste, or disaster are up to $25,000 and/or seizure or forfeiture;	23(1), 24(1) 29(2)(a) and (b) 19(2)(c) and (d) 23(1) 24(1)
	or for failing to make a Master's report on unlawful waste, deposit or distress or for a Master's obstructing or misleading an officer are up to $25,000 and/or seizure or forfeiture.	19(2)(f) 23(1), 24(1) 19(2)(e) 23(1) 24(1)

SELECTED BIBLIOGRAPHY

Alexander, Lewis M., ed. The Law of the Sea. Ohio State
    University Press, 1967.

Andrassy, Juraj. International Law and the Resources of
    the Sea. New York: Columbia University Press, 1970.

Belter, W. G. "Nuclear Waste Management: An Overview of
    Current Practices." Paper presented at the six-
    teenth annual Health Physics Society meeting. New
    York, July 14, 1971.

Borgese, Elizabeth Mann. The Ocean Regime: A Suggested
    Statute. Santa Barbara, Calif.: Center for the
    Study of Democratic Institutions, October 1968.

_____. "The Seas: A Common Heritage," The Center Maga-
    zine 5, no. 2 (March/April 1972).

Bowett, D. W. The Law of the Sea. Dobbs Ferry, N.Y.:
    Oceana, 1967.

Burke, William T. Towards a Better Use of the Ocean.
    Stockholm: Almqvist and Wiksell, 1969.

Burnell, Elaine H., ed. Pacem in Maribus. Santa Barbara,
    Calif.: Center for the Study of Democratic Institu-
    tions, 1970.

Carr, Donald E. Death of Sweet Waters. New York: W. W.
    Norton, 1966.

Cheever, Daniel S. "Marine Science and Ocean Politics,"
    Bulletin of Atomic Scientists, February 1970.

Christol, Carl Q. Oil Pollution of the Marine Environ-
    ment, prepared for the U.S. Senate Public Works Com-
    mittee: Bibliography. Washington, D.C : U.S. Gov-
    ernment Printing Office, 1971.

Christy, Francis T. The Commonwealth in Ocean Fisheries.
    Baltimore: Johns Hopkins Press, 1965.

Commoner, Barry. The Closing Circle. New York: Alfred A. Knopf, 1971.

Cowan, Edward. Oil and Water: The Torrey Canyon Disaster. Philadelphia: J. B. Lippincott, 1968.

Crutchfield, J. A., ed. The Fisheries Problem in Resource Management. Seattle: University of Washington Press, 1965.

Degler, Stanley E. Oil Pollution: Problems and Policies. Cambridge, Mass.: MIT Press, 1971.

Jordan, F. J. E. "Recent Developments in International Environmental Pollution Control," McGill Law Journal, June 1969, pp. 279-311.

Loftas, Tony. The Last Resource: Man's Exploitation of the Oceans. Chicago: Henry Regnery, 1970.

Mackenthun, Kenneth M. The Practice of Water Pollution Biology. Washington, D.C.: U.S. Government Printing Office, 1969.

Marx, Wesley. The Frail Ocean. New York: Ballantine Books, 1967.

Matthews, William H., ed. Man's Impact on Terrestrial and Oceanic Ecosystems. Cambridge, Mass.: MIT Press, 1971.

McDougal, Myres S., and William T. Burke. The Public Order of the Oceans: A Contemporary International Law of the Sea. New Haven: Yale University Press, 1962.

Mero, John L. The Mineral Resources of the Sea. Amsterdam: Elsevier, 1965.

National Academy of Science-National Research Council. The Effects of Atomic Radiation on Oceanography and Fisheries. Washington, D.C., 1957.

_____. "Ocean Pollution: An Examination of the Problem and an Appeal for International Cooperation," San Diego Law Review 7, no. 3 (July 1970).

_____. Official Records of the UN Conference on the Law of the Sea 1958-60. Geneva: United Nations, 1962.

Olson, Theodore A., and Frederick J. Burgess, eds. Pollution and Marine Ecology. New York: Interscience, 1967.

_____. Our Nation and The Sea (Stratton Report). Washington, D.C.: U.S. Government Printing Office, 1969.

_____. Proceedings, Pacem in Maribus-2. Santa Barbara: The Center for the Study of Democratic Institutions, 1971.

Padelford, Norman J. Public Policy for the Sea. Cambridge, Mass.: MIT Press, 1970.

Petrow, Richard. In the Wake of Torrey Canyon. New York: David McKay, 1968.

_____. Report of the Intergovernmental Working Group on Marine Pollution on its Second Session. Ottawa, November 1971.

_____. Report of the Preparatory Committee for the UN Conference on Human Environment: Second Session. Geneva, February 1971.